Core Coaching

Coaching for great performance at work

Sheridan Maguire

DIRECTORY OF SOCIAL CHANGE

Published by
Directory of Social Change
24 Stephenson Way
London NW1 2DP
Tel: 0845 077 7707
Fax: 020 7391 4804
Email: publications@dsc.org.uk
Website: www.dsc.org.uk
from whom further copies and a full books catalogue are available.

Directory of Social Change is a Registered Charity no. 800517
First published 2008

ISBN 978 1 906294 23 6

British Library Cataloguing in Publication Data

A catalogue record for this book is available from the British Library

Cover and text designed by Kate Bass
Typeset by Marlinzo Services, Frome
Printed and bound by Page Bros

All Directory of Social Change departments in London:
0845 077 7707

Directory of Social Change Northern Office
Research: 0151 708 0136

Contents

About the author

Sheridan is a highly effective business performance coach, with a particular interest in organisational leadership development. He has worked extensively across sectors including central and local government, universities, the arts, banking and financial services, the police, the power industry and the NHS (including 1:1 coaching at Chief Executive level).

Sheridan also works with regional and national charities, teachers in secondary schools, and has coached on the government's 14–19 Agenda programme for disaffected young people. He has designed and run group workshops, coach training programmes, senior strategy meetings, facilitated training days and action learning sets and has coached directors and senior executives on a 1:1 basis for over ten years.

Sheridan is a founder-director of Walking With Leaders (WWL) a coaching consultancy specialising in improving business performance through leadership and performance coaching, and helping managers become better coaches in their organisations. WWL is an accredited learning centre for the Institute of Leadership and Management and runs accredited coaching programmes to Level 7 Certificate and Diploma.

He is also a Faculty coach and programme leader for the School of Coaching, one of the UK's most respected coaching training organisations. Sheridan is an accredited coach and assessor for the School's prestigious programme certificated by the University of Strathclyde. He is an associate consultant to Campaign for Leadership at the Work Foundation and CFM Consulting. As is a qualified coaching supervisor Sheridan helps other coaches ensure that they are delivering best value and ethical work for their own clients.

Sheridan has written many articles on coaching in journals including *Managing Best Practice* and the *Journal of Change Management*. With a background in publishing management, Sheridan was previously Head of Publishing at the Work Foundation (formerly the Industrial Society) where he developed the publications division into a major award-winning multi-media business, before becoming a full-time business coach in 1997.

As coach, Sheridan works with senior executives to challenge their current thinking and to help create new opportunities for breakthrough performance at work. Central to this is a strong focus on raising personal awareness and clarity on how the coaching will impact results – not just in the short term, but also in the longer term through personal growth and development.

Contact Sheridan via the publisher or through www.walkingwithleaders.com

Foreword

After more than twenty years in the business I am pleased to report that I no longer get asked whether coaching is a fad. That's the good news. The less good news is that there are still many misconceptions as to what coaching is – and little appreciation of what it can be. Coaching is mostly understood, outside the sports context, as 'Executive Coaching', the provision of coaching by an external professional, or as 'Life Coaching'. Within many places of work coaching is seen as remedial, like the failing student getting 'extra coaching'. Few people understand that coaching is an integral part of the line manager's role and few line managers understand that a significant number of the conversations that they have with their direct reports, either could be, or are, coaching conversations. Frequently, when working with manager or leadership populations to develop coaching skills, coaching is seen as an additional burden, another thing to do in an already busy schedule.

Maybe this is just beginning to change. As the economy tightens, the wiser members of the HR community are turning their attention to ensuring that everything is in place to retain and get the best from those who work in their organisations. And many of those are beginning to appreciate that the coaching ability of the leadership and management populations is a critical factor in this and also in creating a high-performance culture.

An individual in work needs to know three critical things that together make up a large part of the conditions needed for high performance. These are: what to do, how to do it and why. Simply put, establishing 'what to do' is a management activity, the 'why' is largely a leadership activity and the 'how to do it' a coaching activity. Leadership, management and coaching come together in the line manger's remit to create the conditions for high performance.

I recall facilitating a meeting of senior managers where there was a general complaint about the performance and intransigence of the middle managers in their sector – they called it the 'permacore': a frozen stratum. I pointed out that if a level of management is under-performing in an organisation then the place to look is one or two levels up – to the leadership, management and coaching capabilities of their leaders.

By far the largest coaching community in the land is the leadership and management population – and they do not know it. Imagine what would happen if that changed, was acknowledged and if that community really delivered. Imagine the productivity, the effectiveness, the creativity, the learning and joy in the workplace that would follow. Imagine that.

Sheridan, I know, does. I have known him for over ten years and his innate wisdom, humanity and pragmatism are present in this book. I commend it to you.

Myles Downey

Founder of The School of Coaching and author of
Effective Coaching *(Thomson/Texere)*

Acknowledgements

I am indebted to the hundreds of managers and trainee coaches with whom I have worked over the years. I think it was Frank Lloyd Wright who said that an expert was someone who has stopped learning, so to all those who have allowed me to remain 'non-expert', and in the inquiry with them about the possibility of coaching at work, my thanks to you – you know who you are. The same applies to colleagues and friends from The Industrial Society/The Work Foundation: Andrew Forrest and Peter Hill, both of whom gave me valuable feedback on the manuscript; Debra Allcock Tyler, Maria Pemberton, Miki Walleczek, Patrick Burns and Tony Morgan.

I would like to acknowledge Neil Rogers, the voice of my writing conscience, and my business partner Margaret Lloyd who, apart from being a great coach, keeps me grounded in the practical and also has an excellent wine cellar.

Also, the great coaches at the Faculty of the School of Coaching: Virginia Brown, Trevor Waldock, Mike Munro-Turner, David Webster, Jane Meyler, Chris Sheepshanks, Judith Firman, Sue Delafons, Kirsty Leishmann, Nicola Haskins, Julian Tutty, and Myles Downey who – as great coaches do – held a belief in my potential as a coach when it was not at all clear to me and whose passion for coaching is inspirational.

My thanks to editors Lisa Corado and Lucy Muir-Smith, who have been instrumental in guiding this book to print and to publisher John Martin for having faith that it might even sell a few copies.

And finally to my partner Anita and sons Rob and Dunc, patient and accepting in so many ways, my thanks, and at last you can have the computer back.

About the book

This book is primarily for managers who want to improve their own performance, and the performance of their teams (also, coaches who work with managers and teams will find it useful).

The aim of *Core Coaching* is to help managers appreciate that they have a dual role – that of managing *and* coaching – and for them to use that appreciation more effectively in their day-to-day conversations at work. In the Introduction that follows I have explained why I believe coaching to be so important at work, and why it is worth the effort to create coaching cultures in our workplaces.

Chapter 1 is an overview of coaching at work, as a manager and team coach, and of how mentoring fits into development at work, as well as giving a holistic approach to workplace coaching (five-way coaching), ethics and supervision.

Chapter 2 describes eight key areas of capability that the really effective manager or performance coach demonstrates in their work. These eight capabilities make up the acronym STAMINAS, and each is discussed in detail in this section.

Chapter 3 consists of a non-scientific, self-score coaching style questionnaire. Using your understanding of the eight STAMINAS, your answers to this simple questionnaire will help you to identify your own particular coaching style from four main style categories: Creative, Offensive, Relational and Empirical (CORE). Each style is described, with a few pointers about how to develop a more rounded style.

Finally, in Chapter 4, there is a tools and techniques section which describes a number of ways to make your coaching more effective, drawn from my own personal coaching practice and experience.

Introduction

WHY COACHING AT WORK WORKS

Although coaching is rapidly becoming a professional discipline of considerable complexity, underpinned by much psychological research, published books and ethics and standards, at its heart still lies the message of the Greek philosopher, Epicurus:

> There are few better remedies for anxiety than thought. In writing a problem down or airing it in conversation, we let its essential aspects emerge. And, by knowing its character, we remove, if not the problem itself, then its secondary, aggravating characteristics of confusion, displacement and surprise.

It is these 'aggravating characteristics' that cause us all so many problems – fear, doubt, confusion, poor focus, lack of confidence or self-esteem – whether you are a world-class athlete, professional musician, six-year-old child in the school playground, manager or chief executive.

For all of us, one of the biggest 'aggravating characteristics' is other people – the way we think about them, the way we listen to them and the way we have got used to being heard by them. In fact, this is *the* aggravating characteristic which makes ordinary conversations loaded from the very beginning: we simply do not listen to understand or appreciate, or listen without judgement. We listen for the most part simply to respond to be clever, appear knowledgeable, retain position or win in some way. We are ready with advice, instructions, excuses or justifications and this has been our collective experience of conversation since we were each very young. In effect we become imprisoned by these learned responses, each of us living in a world that occurs as shaped by them – and this greatly reduces our capacity to respond to the world as it actually *is*.

A letter to the editor in the international *National Geographic* magazine (March 2008) from the psychoanalyst Paul Heber states:

> My theory is that we do not store stimuli, we only store our responses to stimulus. From age zero and even earlier, we are bombarded by stimuli, so that we constantly respond. We store these responses and they become our subconscious. The stimuli get stored as memories only on the conscious level. The task of psychoanalysis is to help bring the subconscious responses into consciousness, where we are able to take charge of them. As long as they remain in the subconscious, they are in charge of us.

Coaching is definitely *not* psychoanalysis or therapy, but there is a parallel here. Coaching does have a clear and powerful role to play in helping the coachee understand how and why they are responding to certain stimuli – 'aggravating characteristics' – and to develop more effective strategies to achieve their goals. Coaching raises awareness to sharpen perception of occurrences and allows for different, more effective responses.

ICE AND WATER

I sometimes compare a person's thinking to water in ice form – very often it is inflexible and 'frozen' – in this state our capacity to be fully aware, think clearly and to respond with effective agility is diminished. We are stuck in a certain view of things, interpreting events in the same old way and reacting to them in our personal, historic pattern. Telling someone what to do when their thinking is in this state is like chipping away at it with an ice pick (which of course is part of *our* own worldview), in the hope that you will chip off enough ice for the coachee to get to something useful underneath – they might, but figuratively at least, it is a painful process, inelegant and not in the control of the coachee – they aren't holding the ice pick, after all. Besides, how does the wielder of this figurative ice pick know where the best place is to offer their 'help'?

An effective coach will create what I call a *listening space* (more about this later), which in effect allows the ice to thaw and so to become fluid – thinking becomes easier, less constrained and moves with fluidity to make connections it otherwise could not when it was solid. The coach does not wield an ice pick but uses the power of dialogue to create a shift in the coachee's mental state.

So, coaching is not an ordinary conversation. Coaching is an extraordinary conversation: a dialogue based on mutual trust, respect and with only one purpose, the achievement of specific performance goals. Coaching is not easy because it requires us to do something we may not have done for many years – to shut up, empty ourselves of the need to respond and to listen without judgement in order to truly enter into another's worldview. In doing so, we allow them space to enter that world too, but in an enquiring and structured way. Only then can the coach help the coachee to explore their own reality and to find and own their own solutions.

Underpinning any coaching conversation is the fundamental belief that every individual has huge potential which can be unlocked to achieve outstanding personal performance, if only the person could 'get out of their own way'. We are our own worst enemies when it comes to personal performance – who in the world does not have nagging self-doubt, crises of confidence, worries about personal or professional issues, some lurking occasional lack of self-esteem as well as gaps in knowledge and skills? – and these detract from our personal performance.

Coaching is about helping the individual to become focused and engaged and so adapt more quickly and perform more effectively in the moment. The more effectively we can learn, the more quickly we can adapt to circumstances, and this translates spontaneously into far higher levels of performance and goal achievement. Telling people what to do so they can perform better is superficial and leads to small incremental rises in performance in the short term. However, usually it does not help people to learn; learning is fundamentally a *choice* by the learner. You can force people to do something but you can never force people to *choose* to do something – only they have that power – and this lies at the core of intrinsic motivation. So, powerful learning – and therefore powerful performance – is a matter of choice brought about by raised personal awareness, not coercion. As Arthur Schopenhauer said:

> *We learn by rearranging what we know into a more meaningful configuration.*

Generations of world-class performers in every field of human endeavour, including the workplace, know that to achieve their full, extraordinary human potential and to be outstandingly successful, coaching makes all the difference between winning and mediocrity. This occurs only through generating awareness and intrinsic motivation in the coachee, rather than telling them what to do.

Throughout this book, the approach to coaching I espouse is essentially non-directive: helping another to find their own solution, *not* by imposing one's own advice or solution upon them. That does not preclude those times when telling or instructing *is* the best way to help someone else move forward; it simply means that the coach has a mindset of *non-directive intent*, which is a very different place to listen from than that of the teacher, instructor or manager.

Ultimately, no human being can be with another and not, in some way, project subconsciously. Even in total silence we are communicating and influencing the other in subtle and hidden ways. The effective coach (and communicator) will be more aware of what is happening in the space between themselves and the coachee and will notice and use this information to act appropriately in the service of the coachee and their performance goals.

WHY COACHING IS IMPORTANT AT WORK

Work is about the search for daily meaning as well as daily bread, for recognition as well as cash, for astonishment rather than torpor, for a sort of life rather than a Monday to Friday sort of dying.
— Studs Terkel, social anthropologist

Most people spend more time at work than any other activity in their life and many spend the rest of it trying either to forget about it or, if they can't, then worrying about it. Work is seen as a necessary evil by millions of people, the workplace as somewhere to go and freeze-frame their lives for eight hours, every day, before going home and *really* starting to live. This is a tragedy on an epic scale, because the workplace can be made to be exciting and engaging and work can made to be challenging and meaningful, giving individuals a real sense of personal purpose and satisfaction.

It is managers who are accountable for getting the best results that they can from their staff and, on the whole, the results are mediocre. Generally speaking, this is not because they don't try, or don't have the best interests of their staff or organisation at heart. It is because they don't know how to use managing as a way to get the best from people. This is not surprising, as managing is *not* the conversation to get the best from people – coaching is!

Coaching is specifically designed as a conversation to improve performance, in whatever walk of life. At work, it is primarily the manager who has the coaching role, and yet they spend most of the time telling people what to do instead of helping them see for themselves what they could do. This shift of emphasis – from telling to facilitating – is crucial, as it engages ownership, free thinking and responsibility to act. These are the hallmarks of the learning organisation: one which nurtures and harnesses individual learning in the service of organisational goals. Even in the twenty-first century we still have a tendency to ignore the axiom, 'With every pair of hands you get a free brain'. Yet we all know that the one main competitive advantage that any organisation has over its competitors is its people. As Arie de Geus, business strategist and former corporate planning director at Shell, said:

> *The ability to learn faster than the competition is often the only sustainable competitive advantage a company can have.*

The word 'sustainable' is important: tell someone what to do and they will be back the next day with another question to be answered, and often it is the wrong question. Constantly reinventing the wheel and creating organisational bottlenecks is not a sustainable practice. It merely perpetuates the status quo, entrenches behaviours and stifles creative thinking and action.

Managers can break through this stagnation by generating a different kind of conversation that is performance-focused, engaging and allows others to be responsible and take action. These conversations tap into people's innate talent, personal desire for achievement and sense of ownership. Everyone wants to be great, show up well, enjoy their working life and be successful. It is the manager's role and responsibility to make that happen in the service of their organisation, stakeholders and staff. And coaching is the way to do it.

1 Managers coaching at work

1.1 THE MANAGER AS COACH

How coaching fits in the organisation

We all want to find meaning and value in our work and to feel a sense of purpose and self-esteem. In this day and age, this calls upon a very different management style. Managing people in the traditional sense just doesn't work any more. Indeed, the word 'manager' is derived from the Italian word *maneggiare:* to control or train, especially horses. 'Carrot and stick' might have worked in organisations 20 or 30 years ago, but not in the twenty-first century. The issue of control is critical: it is a basic human driver to 'be in control', and anything that might contribute to a sense of loss of control – for example, suspending one's values, opinions or judgements when listening authentically to someone else – is a tough development issue for nearly all of us.

Coaching is a style of conversation that is more open, honest and engaging. It is geared towards helping people to think and perform for themselves, rather than rein them in. However, for coaching to succeed in organisations, it must be *integrated into everyday usage and language,* and it must be seen and heard to be integrated through the behaviours of the most senior managers.

Isn't coaching just another management fad?

In a way, it is the other way around. Coaching has been the way in which interested and empathetic individuals have helped and developed others for many thousands of years. For as long as there have been human parents and children, there has been some form of coaching. The concept of organisational management is far more recent, and evolved with the emergence of procedures and rules that are necessary to stop an organisation from sliding into chaos. So, management is about boundaries, while coaching is about growth. The difficult trick for the manager is to separate out these two conversations: maintaining appropriate boundaries (which clearly organisations need to operate effectively), while encouraging learning and development within these boundaries.

The question for every manager is: how do I maintain appropriate boundaries (managing) and create an environment for learning, adaptation, agility and action (coaching) at the same time?

The manager's role

The manager has two clear roles to perform simultaneously – managing and coaching. The clearer they can separate or distinguish between these roles, the more effective they can be. This is easy to say, but not so easy to do.

Managing

Managers are accountable for delivering on their objectives through strategic leadership (the processes or systems that all agree will move the organisation towards its stated destination) and the appropriate and effective use of the resources at their disposal. It is entirely appropriate for managers to have conversations around:

- performance management
- targets and setting goals
- delegation
- accountability
- organising and monitoring resources
- evaluation and measurement
- compliance with procedural and behavioural norms.

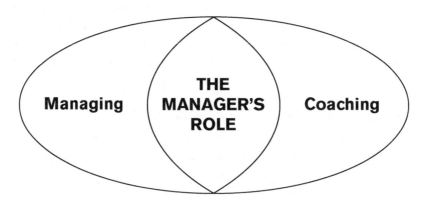

Management conversations are all about the *what* of the individual's level of performance, as judged by the standards set by the organisation. By their nature there is an element of judgement and imposition about them. Management conversations are generally centred in the manager's own experience of the overall context, their departmental and personal objectives and those of the coachee or subordinate. They will have a legitimate agenda and expectation around performance, standards, the accountability of the coachee and cultural norms ('the way we behave and have conversations around here'). In this regard, managers have a clear and legitimate agenda, some aspects of which may seem to fly in the face of simultaneously acting as manager-coach.

Coaching

Coaching conversations are all about enhancing the individual's awareness of *how* they can achieve optimum performance. They are about helping the person to play the very best game they can (within the rules). This is a very different type of conversation, focusing on the manager's personal leadership and their capacity to draw out and nurture the innate talent of their people through:

- enabling
- responsibility
- awareness
- intrinsic motivation
- self-confidence
- personal choice
- engaging discretionary effort.

There is no element of judgement, criticism or imposition in a coaching conversation. The purpose is only and always to help the coachee to raise their level of awareness around a task or issue in a motivating and energetic way, so that they are able to see more ways forward than before and are inspired to act through their own self-discovery. Coaching conversations are generally centred in the coachee's experience: what they are aware of, feeling, learning and experiencing and what they can do for themselves to improve and achieve more.

Obviously, managing and coaching conversations will overlap to a degree. Sometimes the manager-coach will have to impose 'rules' which might constrain the coaching, or help the coachee to understand that the ideas they have come up with won't work for specific contextual reasons. You cannot 'coach out' from other people information you know and which they don't – you just have to tell them, otherwise it is unhelpful.

Sometimes the manager will have to direct the conversation to a particular performance issue, target or goal on which the coachee needs to work. This is perfectly appropriate in the management role. However, once directed to that place, the conversation should then focus back on what the coachee can do for themselves, not what the manager thinks the coachee should be doing about it. Similarly, the manager-coach will have views or feedback which might be useful for the person to know in order to increase the data – and so the self-awareness – available to them. The difficulty is that the manager and the coach in this conversation *are the same person* and it takes time and practice to become skilled at the duality. The conversations may overlap, but they are *distinct*.

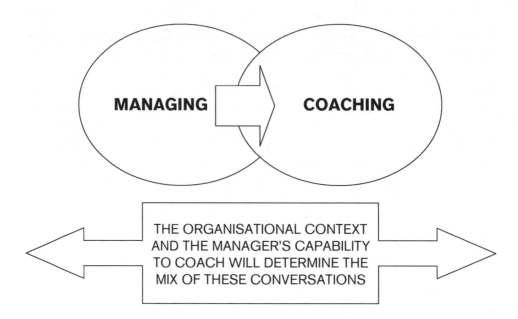

MANAGING → COACHING

THE ORGANISATIONAL CONTEXT AND THE MANAGER'S CAPABILITY TO COACH WILL DETERMINE THE MIX OF THESE CONVERSATIONS

Focus on the manager's experience	*Focus on the coachee's experience*
• more centred in their own experience	• more centred in the coachee's experience
• strategic leadership	• personal leadership
• focus on context	• focus on content
• narrower focus	• wideangle lens
• seeks decisions	• elicits choices
• personal agenda	• no personal agenda
• transactional	• relational
• more assertive	• more allowing
• holds the reins	• gives the horse its head

There are hidden rules in every workplace which are never discussed but which nevertheless form part of the prevailing culture, such as:

- teamwork is espoused but personal performance is rewarded;
- values such as learning and honesty are promoted but often the perceived personal price is too high;
- learning is a luxury that no one can afford.

These rules reflect enlightened self-interest, and are powerful organisational drivers of behaviour which are buried beneath the surface and deeply immersed in the culture of the organisation. The new manager's role must be to realign the hidden rules to meet organisational objectives. For the most part managers are driven, like everyone else, by these deeper and unspoken behavioural drivers. To be an effective manager-coach is to have the courage to surface, challenge and rewrite ineffective or outmoded values, rules or attitudes that stifle potential, growth and development – both their own and those of others.

This is both the challenge and the possibility that coaching can bring to the workplace. The coach's role is to unlock the huge reservoir of potential, energy, creativity and enjoyment in the workplace and then, as manager, to focus that potential towards the achievement of organisational objectives and individual development.

Blocks to coaching in organisations

Some blocks to coaching might include the following:

Lack of genuine commitment from the top

Often coaching is regarded as something that 'is done to staff' to get them to perform better. This is not coaching, it is manipulation, and people will smell a rat in 10 seconds flat. For coaching to succeed, it must be *integrated into everyday usage and language*, and it must be seen and heard to be integrated through the beliefs, attitudes and behaviours of senior managers downwards.

Coaching is regarded as a performance management tool

Performance *management* is a *management* issue. *Performance* is a *coaching* issue, and the two are often confused, with lack of clarity, suspicion and mixed agendas as a consequence. When managers are measuring and monitoring, reviewing and setting targets, they are not coaching, they are managing. Coaching should never replace the essential elements of the line manager's role, which include, for example, clarity about objectives, structure, procedures, monitoring and measuring and compliance issues.

Managers go on a one or two-day coaching programme and, hey presto, they're coaches

In short: they aren't. They have just started a conversation for personal growth for themselves and their people, requiring long-term commitment, continuous learning and a willingness to suspend judgement. Many, probably most, managers will find this difficult to follow through without ongoing coaching and supporting processes such as supervision, monitoring and evaluation, which are often lacking.

Return on Investment short-termism

There is cost associated with introducing coaching into organisations, particularly training and lost-opportunity costs. It is of course absolutely appropriate that every effort is made to evaluate the effectiveness of any coaching initiative. However, coaching is not just a quick hit (although it can be), it is also an investment in the future of the organisation and, like any investment, it takes time to grow. Therefore, evaluating return on investment needs to take both the short term and longer term in view, and it may not always be simple to measure.

We tend not to look at long-term benefits when measuring return on investment, neither do we usually consider the benefits of avoiding potential negative outcomes which otherwise might have occurred. It may be hard to put a specific measure on increased creativity, personal satisfaction and job fulfilment, a more responsible attitude and a sense of intrinsic motivation, but coaching can contribute hugely to these things and make a real impact on the way that individuals do their jobs and how people work together. Also, data such as employee surveys, external evaluations, retention and promotion rates, absence and sickness, customer satisfaction surveys and specific measured results all add hard measures to build a rounded picture of the positive impact of coaching in the organisation, and this data will become more meaningful over time.

The organisational culture is unsupportive

Even if coaching is superficially espoused, underneath, the culture is often one of machismo, short-termism and looking good at the expense of others. The introduction of coaching as a style of conversation into an organisation is a long-term commitment to developing a culture of openness, empowerment, personal choice and responsibility. After centuries of the individual and organisational paradigm that puts 'I' ahead of 'we', it's not surprising that personal agendas crop up in the middle of change initiatives to sabotage them and return the organisation to its status quo.

Lack of clarity about what the organisation can expect from coaching

Effective coaching conversations can transform an organisation and the way that it works – permanently. So, it is important to have some hard measures and firm expectations of what to expect at the individual, team and organisational levels. Clearly, a lack of clarity around what coaching is and isn't, how it will alter leadership and management style, and what impact it will have on the way that people work and have conversations is going to have an impact on effectiveness. Some people or teams will adapt more quickly to change than others, whose inertia can slow or even halt the process.

To draw a loose parallel, it is a bit like changing the operating system of a computer. My personal computer has Microsoft Vista as its operating system. This software is at the heart of the machine, dictating how the computer functions: nothing will work without the operating system, which dictates the machine's way of working and its 'operational rules'. It is also the bridge that links programmes together and creates a coherent whole. To type this book, I have installed a Microsoft Office software package 'on top' of the operating system. This additional software is also essential, as this software allows me to use the computer effectively and achieve the desired results – one would not give the result without the other. But the Vista operating system permeates the whole machine; it runs Microsoft Office software, so I can type this manuscript, but

Vista also runs games, email packages, anti-virus software and anything else one wants to add.

In a sense, the operating system is the *being* of the machine (*what* it is) while the additional software packages are the *doing* of the machine (*how* it is). For many years the 'operating system' of organisations has been the mindset and language of management, dominating every aspect of the machine. Now in the twenty-first century we are seeing the mindset and language of coaching beginning to supersede. The operating system (management) is still there – it has to be, there would be no way to run the machine without it – but it is the additional programme called coaching which is permeating deeper and deeper into the system.

As the business and commercial world becomes ever more complex, so people at work both need and demand ever more flexible approaches that encourage adaptability and creativity and which reflect and encourage individual talent and choice. Consider all the management conversations that happen on a daily basis at work: targets, compliance, procedures, measuring and monitoring and so on. What percentage is that of the whole? Perhaps it might be 40 or 50%, or even more? Then look at the amount of intervention the referee has during, say, a football match as a percentage of the total game – perhaps a maximum of five or six minutes out of 90 minutes' play – that is less than 10%. The game is still rigorously controlled, the rules are crystal clear, but the vast majority of the time is spent playing the game, not controlling it. A great game and results lie in the players playing, not the referee refereeing (but note that a great game will always have had a really good referee).

One might say that this is because football (or any game) is a spectator sport and too much intervention by the referee would make it boring. Well, work is a spectator sport, too. Every day we are watched by our colleagues, customers, shareholders, suppliers – it is just that in this case, the 'referees' (managers) are also on the field of play, as part of the game. Managers have to find a way of distinguishing when they need to play referee (nearer to 10% of the game) and when they need to play on-pitch coach (nearer to 90% of the game). As mentioned above, this is a considerable shift in mindset for managers; the challenge is eloquently captured in this quote:

> *Everyone must change. The change will go deeper than technique. It touches not merely what managers do but who they are. Not just their sense of the task, but their sense of themselves. Not just what they know but how they think. Not just their way of seeing the world, but their way of living in the world.* — James Champy, *Re-Engineering Management*, pp. 9–10

1.2 FIVE-WAY COACHING

One useful model for coaching in the organisation is five-way coaching. In this model, the manager-coach has five different focuses of attention, depending on the circumstances. This model demonstrates the holistic nature of coaching – that is, when speaking with:

- senior colleagues;
- colleagues in the organisation;
- those reporting to you;
- clients, stakeholders, customers;
- oneself (i.e. one's own reflections, thoughts, intuition and so on).

The individual can be more effective in their role by using coaching skills to leverage the conversation and make it count.

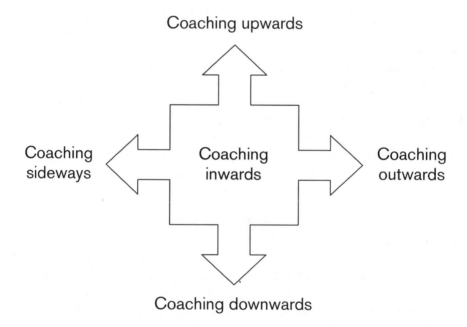

Coaching upwards

Coaching sideways   Coaching inwards   Coaching outwards

Coaching downwards

The five-way coaching model shows how coaching can represent the operating system of the individual manager, with 'managing' as just one of the conversations (although an extremely important one) available for their use. Other conversations 'run' by coaching could be, for example:

- learning and development or appraisal;
- conflict resolution;
- sales and marketing;
- customer contact or complaints and service handling;
- relationship building;
- team meetings or team-building;

- negotiation;
- influencing and persuading.

Coaching upwards

Effective managers will use their skills to listen and frame questions in order to influence and have an impact on decisions made at the levels above themselves. Effective and appropriate questions demonstrate both committed interest and incisive thinking, and these are more likely to engender collaboration rather than command from above. Coaching upwards involves an appreciation of the other person's situation, which is not only factually accurate, but also pays attention to the person's needs and feelings (including their fears).

EXAMPLE: A COACHING MODEL FOR INFLUENCING UPWARDS

Context:
- persuading your line manager to support you or release resources
- getting senior colleagues to appreciate your views more than they do now

Clarity:
- What do I want from this conversation?
- What would be an acceptable compromise for me?
- What does the other person think/feel/want about this issue?

Be specific and transparent:
- I'd like to speak with you about . . . /Can we discuss this issue . . .
- The facts are these . . . /The evidence shows that . . .
- avoid emotion or feelings at this stage – remain factual

Create a clearing:
- What are your views on this? How do you feel about the issue/problem?
- What is your take on this issue? What are your thoughts?
- What outcomes/outputs would help you/give you what you want?
- My understanding is that you need X/Y result – is that correct?

Enrol:
- I can deliver on X/Y if you can help me with resources A, B . . .
- What if I could promise you that outcome – could you offer me some additional time/help/people . . . if you know it would give you the outcome you want?

The following questions are useful when appreciating another's viewpoint.

- What are the facts?
- What do they want?
- What do they need?
- What do they feel about this issue?
- What are their concerns or anxieties about this issue?

Then you need to consider what you want from the conversation.

- What result do I want?
- What result do I need?
- What compromise am I willing to make between what I need and what I want?
- What would success look and sounds like for me/for them?

Finally, pay attention to what would be advantageous mutually ('win–win'). This gives a framework for influencing conversations which benefits both parties.

Coaching sideways

Managers have colleagues across the organisation and they will need to influence and persuade them to cooperate in cross-functional working, collaborative projects and suchlike. Through listening and asking questions that create an appreciative environment with colleagues, for example in the model given above, managers can create new and more engaging relationships with fellow workers. Much of this is to do with creating a different kind of listening, as mentioned earlier, which fosters more honest, open and authentic relationships. It is these new relationships which are the foundation of improved organisational performance.

Coaching outwards

All organisations have suppliers, strategic partnerships and the need to recruit the best people. Effective managers will have the capability to use coaching as a vehicle to demonstrate clear communication, clarity of purpose, a creative and flexible approach to working with people and, above all, a genuine desire to improve relationships and get results. In these days of high competition and slimmer margins, it is vital to maintain competitive advantage, and the only way to do this is through conversation. It is those managers who are skilled at creating conversations which have purpose, clarity, understanding, appreciation and are geared to results who will be the corporate champions of the twenty-first century.

Coaching downwards

Effective managers are those who get the very best from their employees and who care for the individuals as well as for the results that they achieve. As previously mentioned, it is very important to distinguish between the two conversations – managing and coaching – within the line manager's role. They have different but linked agendas, and the more clearly the manager can distinguish between them in their own mind, the more effective they will be at having both management and coaching conversations.

Management conversations are primarily about rules and procedure, and coaching conversations are about 'being on court' – getting the most out of every working day and eliciting maximum discretionary effort through intrinsic motivation.

EXAMPLE 1: USING A COACHING STYLE FOR PERFORMANCE MANAGEMENT CONVERSATIONS

Context:

- monthly one-to-ones or appraisals
- performance target reviews
- project reviews

Clarity of purpose:

- specific purpose and intended outcomes: This meeting is intended to... and the outcomes I am looking for as manager are...
- What would you like to get from this meeting...?

Reviewing the past:

- Tell me about your accomplishments since we last met.
- What went especially well? How do you feel about that?
- What are the key things you think you have learnt?
- If you could do something differently now, what would it be?
- What might stop you from doing that?

Generating the future:

- If you knew you were unstoppable, what would be your next step?
- What specifically do you want to achieve next around this issue?
- What goals/targets/milestones do you think appropriate or possible?
- What will be your success measures?
- What would be the perfect result?

Supporting the commitment:

- Who needs to know?
- Who could support you and how would they do that?
- What requests do you need to make of whom to move forward?
- What might get in your way and what will you do about that?
- How do you want me to support you?

Collaborative feedback:

- How could this session have been better for you (and me)?
- In what way could we improve the way we work together?
- Is there anything else you would like to say to complete this conversation?

EXAMPLE 2: A COACHING MODEL FOR RUNNING TEAM MEETINGS

Context:

- monthly team meetings
- team briefings
- project meetings
- board meetings

Clarity of purpose:

- specific purpose and intended outcomes: This meeting is intended to... and the outcomes I am looking for as manager are...
- What would you like to get from this meeting?

Create a clearing:

- What have been our successes this week/month?
- What has worked particularly well?
- What stands out as a positive moment for you personally?
- seek positive moments and examples from every person

Give information:

- The news is ... /The decision has been taken to... and so on.
- If giving a brief, ensure that you demonstrate alignment with management decisions, even if you disagree in private.

Get feedback and facilitate group sharing:

- What are your thoughts on this ... /What do you think about that...?
- How do you feel about.../What is your reaction to...?

(For detail on the GROW model below, see Structuring in Chapter 2.)

Purpose (**G**ROW):

- As a team, what do we see now as any issues or problems that might stop us performing at our best? What are our issues/concerns?
- What do we need to tackle first... /What's urgent and what's important?
- What do we need to leave this meeting with? (actions, agreements, requests, commitments)

What's the current reality around this issue/problem? (G**R**OW)

- Who/what/how/when/why...?
- What are we assuming?
- What might be going on?
- What do others want/need/feel, and so on?
- split the team into small groups for this, if there is enough time.

(Continued)

What could we do? (GR**O**W):

- What are our options?
- What haven't we done?
- What would we do if we had no fear of failure?
- What would our competitors or worst enemy like us to do?
- What are the pros and cons?
- What have we missed?
- use additional processes such as force-field analysis, brainstorming and so on.

What will happen next (GRO**W**):

- Who specifically in the team will do what by when?
- What is their specific measurable result, what help do they need and how will they get it?
- Do these agreed actions meet our need and if not, what do we need to do?

Coaching inwards

Take rest. A field that has rested gives a beautiful crop. — Ovid

Self-coaching is a powerful life skill. It requires high levels of self-awareness and focused concentration and is characteristic of very high performance. It is an art which can be practised and developed through coaching others, being coached and individual practice.

Take a little time out from the hectic daily schedule for yourself to reflect, take stock and view situations with objectivity. You may do this already, but I suggest making a virtue out of the practice. I know of one very senior manager who was in charge of a large manufacturing complex, with extraordinary demands on his time. Yet every day at lunchtime he would shut his door and be incommunicado for 30 minutes while he quietly sat and thought through issues and concerns. He told me that this 30 minutes allowed him to become focused, relaxed, clearer in thought and more capable in action. He found the time spent in quiet thought paid huge personal performance dividends. (The 'NIP and TUCK' model is a simple model for self-coaching – see p. 116 for more information on how this process works.)

1.3 COACHING TEAMS

Definition

What is the definition of a team? There are a number of different views and my personal one is:

> *A self-sustaining learning community, based on fundamental mutuality and accountability, which takes purposeful action to achieve its goals.*

Teasing that definition apart, there are a number of words that imply certain behaviours or processes in a high-performing team. The following questions can be used to elicit from individual team members the context and culture that underpins the team's current performance. (For an organisational diagnostic, substitute the word 'organisation' for 'team'.)

Self-sustaining:

- How is the team context regularly and openly reviewed?
- What is the process (if any) for openly and fully discussing the undiscussable within the team?
- What are the ground rules, *modus operandi*, team processes?
- Do they work and how often are they reviewed for effectiveness?
- What degree of trust is there in evidence through individual behaviours?

Learning community:

- How open and honest is everyone about mistakes – is the truth spoken and are breakdowns declared immediately, without fear of recrimination or loss of face?
- How are lessons regularly learnt and shared through the team?
- What is the process for feedback for both individuals and the team?
- How is personal and team development catered for, and how does this align with personal accountabilities?
- What are the team's fundamental strengths and areas for improvement?

Fundamental mutuality and accountability:

- To what degree is every team member included, able to influence and made to feel regarded and respected – that is, what is the degree to which they can have their say, have their way and be OK?
- What is the expression of fun and energy through everyday actions and team interventions?
- What unique practices or drills does the team have which set it apart from others?
- Are personal accountabilities absolutely clear?
- What is the level of trust across the team?

Purposeful action:

- To what degree does everyone behave responsibly?
- Are requests and promises regularly made and clearly distinguished?
- What level of support is freely offered and accepted in the team?
- How effective is the team in terms of communicating with itself and others, both within and outside the organisation?
- When action stops, where is the breakdown generally occurring in the team, in the organisation or elsewhere?
- How are such breakdowns addressed at the moment?

Achieve its goals:

- Does every team member have absolute clarity about why they are there and what success means in terms of measurable results?
- What is the team vision? Can everyone state it clearly and unambiguously?
- Is success freely celebrated and are all contributions fully acknowledged?
- How does the leader show up in the team? What are their strengths and areas for development? How do their behaviours impact the team?

What does a group of people need to do, and how do they need to be, in order to achieve these things and perform as an outstanding team? The challenge for the team coach is that individuals in the team are just that – individuals – and each will have their own values, beliefs, agendas and ways of succeeding. To generate true team performance – which can be far greater than the sum of the individual performances – everyone in the team needs to be aligned both behaviourally and attitudinally, but not to the extent that the individuals lose their individuality. A great team consists of inventive human beings, not robots.

The team coaching process

What's the difference between team coaching and team facilitation? I make a distinction in defining team facilitation as *helping a team to collect their thoughts to achieve a specific outcome*, while defining team coaching as *helping a team to discover their thoughts to achieve breakthrough results*. The key distinction is between *collect* thoughts and *discover* them, implying that coaching can be a deeper, more inventive and non-linear process – and certainly more challenging.

The coach needs to understand the individuals in the team and over time, reveal to the team the dynamics between them. The team coach has to be mindful of the fact that there is always one more personality in the room than there are individuals, for the team *itself* has its own personality. Watching for the interactions between different team members, as well as seeing the team as a whole, is complex, challenging and extremely rewarding. By bringing differences to the surface, declaring breakdowns when they occur and revealing why they occurred, the coach can bring the team to a deeper awareness of themselves/itself – both as individuals and as one individual (in this case, the team).

A typical team coaching process usually commences with an initial in-depth briefing with the client (who may or may not be the team leader), and the team leader (if another person) about the purpose of the coaching, the intended result and how it will be measured and monitored, as well as any logistical issues. The process will look something like this:

1) Interview each team member separately, eliciting honest answers around some of the key questions posed under the five headings above.

2) At the first team coaching session, give the team the anonymised feedback, divided into any key emergent themes, and seek their views. Have the team create their own 'team climate' chart of, for example, eight to 10 key areas for improvement, which they choose for themselves as a team. Ensure that ground rules are aligned and kept to for all subsequent sessions. Revisit the ground rules at the start of each subsequent session.

3) Within the context of the team's goals, review the team's progress against the climate chart at each session: what is improving, what is not moving, and discover why.

4) At each subsequent session, review progress towards goals and actions taken and/or breakdowns encountered. The breakdowns are a gift – they allow for conversations that reflect on every aspect of relationship and communication in the team and beyond.

These conversations will be tough to begin with, as individuals attempt to conceal their own fears, embarrassment and reveal their need to justify themselves, judge their peers and opinionate – as though *any* of that will forward purposeful action!

Evolution of the team

The evolution of a team is well documented, perhaps most notably by Bruce Tuckman, whose team dynamic model has become the standard yardstick for team development. The following figure shows the normal sequence of the Tuckman model.

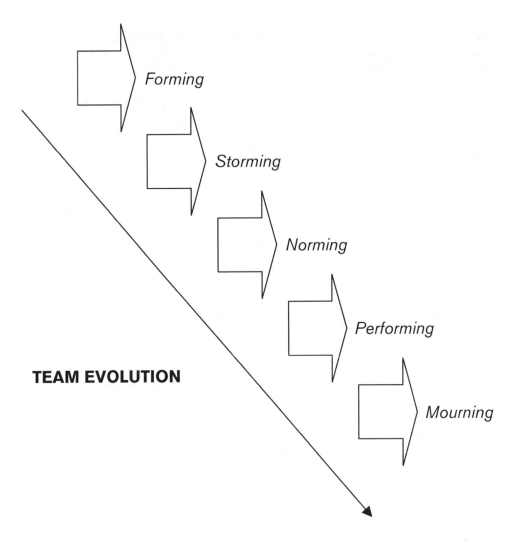

TEAM EVOLUTION

The *Forming* stage is typified by polite wariness, as new team members work out ways of becoming included in the team 'conversation' without too much personal commitment. It is a time of hidden agendas and correctness, as each person gets on with the others by agreeing and being superficially aligned. This usually is not the case, and beneath the surface there is dissent, non-alignment, unspoken frustration and untold truths. M. Scott Peck, the renowned expert in community building, calls this stage 'pseudo-community'.

The *Storming* stage is typified by individuals asserting their individuality and need to be right about things. Different camps usually emerge, as sub-leaders emerge to test the leader and these then fight it out more or less politely according to the culture of the team or organisation. The lid is off the pressure cooker and the steam flies about with the hiss of hot air. This can become unpleasant and personal, and sooner or later the leader or the team as a whole will sit on the pressure cooker lid, bottle up the issues that seem to threaten the team and settle into 'normality'. This is the *Norming* stage, a fairly robust community out of which performance, in theory at least, emerges.

It would be easy for the coach to assume that their work was nearing completion once the team appears to be norming, yet this is the point of most challenge and leverage in the team. The team usually slips back into a more relational and organised version of Forming, rather than be confronted by the more difficult and most challenging side of Storming. After all, there is still pressure in the cooker – all the team has done is to slam on the lid and pretend all is now well. However, beneath the surface is the unspoken fear of confronting what Scott Peck calls 'emptiness'. This is the point of letting go – of the need to have answers, to be right, to opinionate, judge, blame or help others (in order to feel good about oneself). It is at this stage that the lid is removed from the pressure cooker, the steam dissipates, and what is left? With skilful, minimum facilitation at this point, the coach can help the team to have authentic, open and honest conversations with and for each other, opening the door to the final stage, Performing.

At this stage, the team is theoretically performing at a high level. This is characterised by high levels of mutual trust and support, an absolute focus on the task, deeply held personal accountability and clear dialogues that are unambiguous and create clear individual commitments and promises. People keep their word. This generates a lot of energy and enthusiasm and raises spirits – team members of a high-performing team have a lot of fun as well as success. No wonder Scott Peck, who labels this stage of community-building 'community', attaches another label to it: 'glory'. To belong to such a team and to play one's part in its outstanding success is indeed glorious.

A fifth stage, *Mourning*, is added occasionally to the Tuckman model. It is certainly the case that disbanding a high-performance team can be a highly emotional time for the team members, who have come to trust each other so implicitly.

The coach's role

The coach's role is to help the team make the journey from pseudo-community to community, and to ensure not only that the team learns as much as it can from the journey about itself as an individual, but that the individuals understand their role within it.

Transparency
The coach has no hidden agendas. When coaching teams, I always let them know what they might be in for by explaining the process. Everyone understands it

intellectually, but it is amazing just how unaware we all are of our tendency to keep reverting to type and then becoming surprised or upset when we find ourselves in chaos! I will point out to them their behaviours and ask where we are in the model, in order to raise team awareness.

Context

It is so easy for a team to get fixed on the present task and not be able to see the wood for the trees. Being fixed on the present task is actually being stuck in the past. The task or problem occurred in the past and normally that is where we go to find an answer, despite the fact that it is history. As the saying goes: if you always do what you have always done, you will always get what you have always got. That will not be enough to survive in this competitive world.

> The significant problems we have created ... cannot be solved at the same level of thinking we were at when we created them.   — Albert Einstein

We tend to go into the past for solutions, even for new ideas and forecasting, as we gravitate towards the things that we know, understand and accord with our current view of the world (which is historic as soon as we have thought it). One of the roles of the team coach is to create a listening environment that allows the team to move behind the historic content of their thinking to the present *context* which is driving it. It is the 'why are we here?' question, concerned with shared values and grounded in a clear vision. In a sense, it is moving from 'what are we doing together?' to 'who are we being together?', which is an altogether deeper enquiry. This type of ongoing enquiry generates the context from which the team operates and allows for a different kind of dialogue to occur in the team, as nothing is undiscussable or preserved in aspic. It allows for faster, more connected team thinking.

In his book *Synchronicity: The Inner Path of Leadership*, Joseph Jaworski describes some of the thinking behind the work on dialogue by the renowned physicist Professor David Bohm. Bohm described how an individual's personal worldview creates deep assumptions which then drive their own thinking, a bit like a computer virus taking over a program. This creates a situation in which our understanding of each other is fragmented. As Bohm put it:

> Ordinary thought in society is incoherent – it's going in all sorts of directions, cancelling each other out.   — The Essential David Bohm, p. 309

Jaworski explains:

> If people were to think together in a coherent way, it would have tremendous power. If there was an opportunity for sustained dialogue over a period of time, we would have coherent movement of thought, not only at the conscious level we all recognize, but even more importantly at the tacit level, the

unspoken level which cannot be described. Dialogue does not require people to agree with each other. Instead, it encourages people to participate in a pool of shared meaning that leads to aligned action. — *Synchronicity*, p. 111

Feedback

The team coach needs to reflect to the team regularly their behaviours according to agreed ground rules. This might include periodic one-to-ones with the coach, or better still, that the team organises their own process for regular team feedback to each other. Again, the ground rules will apply.

Challenge

The team coach must never shy away from challenging behaviours that are contrary to the team's chosen way of working. Moreover, the coach will see or hear things in the team which others are unaware of or consider undiscussable and the coach should raise these, if they consider it appropriate.

Coaching through breakdowns

There will be many powerful opportunities in the development of the team for the team coach to intervene and make observations about the group dynamics or individual behaviour. The coach is in the uniquely privileged position of being both outside the group yet accepted and trusted by those within it. It is up to the coach to:

- ensure every view is heard and understood and appreciated;
- encourage disagreement and investigative dialogue;
- state the issue as simply and succinctly as possible;
- encourage bold and imaginative thinking around the issue;
- ensure all are aligned to the team goal or outcome;
- use a structure such as GROW to create dialogue for action;
- hold a strong line around action – there should be no excuses for actions not completed, although of course there will be a number of reasons. What matters is: what is the learning; what is the individual and team commitment to re-engage in action; and what are the next steps?

When coaching through breakdowns, either individually or with teams, focus on questions such as the following.

- What happened?
- What effect has this had on you/the team/customers, and so on?
- What are you now feeling or thinking?
- What do you think that the team/customers are thinking or feeling?
- What have you learned?
- What could or would you do differently with the benefit of hindsight?
- What are you committed to doing now?

Ensuring inclusion

Everyone has a need to feel that they belong. We may be individuals, but our individualism can be expressed only within the culture of a group, otherwise there is no one else to witness or relate to our own individuality. In terms of the team, this is about fundamental mutuality and accountability. The coach needs to be continually aware of every individual and how they are relating to the team as a whole. This requires vigilance and sensitivity on the part of the coach. Some inclusion issues are best addressed in the group, and others on a one-to-one basis initially, before the individual shares it with the team.

Occasionally the coach might want to introduce a process to allow the team to discuss inclusion explicitly. One simple method is team contribution scoring. This is a simple and useful method of demonstrating how members rate their own involvement in the performance of the team during or after a meeting or team activity.

The process

Draw a grid on a flipchart and have each team member place two marks on the grid. One mark – say, in black pen – represents the current *team* performance against agreed meetings criteria such as sharing, inclusion, appreciation, acknowledgement, listening to others and so on. The second mark represents where each team member feels they are *personally* in terms of their own contribution to the discussion.

Team contribution scoring

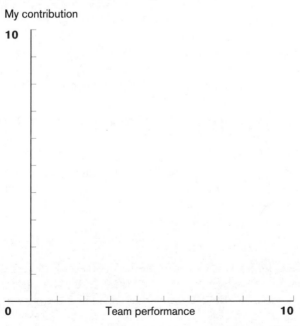

My contribution

10

0   Team performance   10

CASE STUDY

I was asked by the sales team manager in a medium-sized service organisation to help the team come up with a definitive team vision and some new ways of working towards their team objectives. The team was under pressure to improve their performance during a turbulent time of change for the organisation. The team leader held the budget and so represented the client as well as the team.

I began by talking at length with the manager. He was evidently depressed, felt overworked and unsupported by his team of six, most of whom were considerably younger and less experienced than himself. He told me that he knew exactly what needed to be done and was frustrated by the team's apparent lack of ability to deliver, despite all the 'hand-holding and advice' he kept giving them. He also felt very unsupported by and isolated from his own line manager, the sales director.

I checked with him that he understood the process that he would certainly receive feedback about his own leadership style and behaviours, which could be challenging for him. He affirmed that all feedback he received would be accepted as valuable learning for him.

I then talked to the team individually. What emerged was a picture of a team with low morale and poor sense of personal responsibility, not well trained and verbally bullied – although subtly – by their manager. They felt that he was passing his frustrations on to them, behaving dictatorially and not utilising their talents. They too felt unsupported by the organisation, but did feel that the manager did what he could to represent them in the best light at director meetings.

The feedback concerning the manager's style and behaviours around the team was so strong that, after ensuring it was not identifiable to any one team member, I met again with the manager before setting a date for the team workshop. He first denied it was true, and then said that it was excusable because of recent circumstances. Finally he conceded that he had always 'managed' in this way and didn't know how to be different, and he became upset.

Coach: Given your commitment to achieving the team's objectives and your stated wish for the team to work more effectively, where do you want this conversation to go now?

Manager: I'd like to work out how I can work with my team so I understand what effect my behaviours are having on them. Maybe some simple ground rules or something.

Coach: How would you like to do that?

Manager: Well, I guess I could ask them.

A few minutes' further conversation and he decided to get the team together there and then. He did so and explained that he had received some tough feedback about his leadership style and that he wanted to establish some ways of working together as a team, ahead of the workshop, to be reviewed at that time.

He went on to say how he felt about the feedback and (just about) avoided making excuses for himself. The team were very supportive and appreciative of their manager and they worked together quickly to produce a few ground rules about behaviours, running both ways, which proved to be a successful stepping-stone into the workshop a month later.

The workshop was a useful opportunity to review progress and it was evident that communication was more effective on both sides. The manager had 'loosened up' a little, was delegating more and was surprised to find more talent in his team than he imagined. The team came up with a neat team vision, some key operating principles and identified seven areas of improvement, each championed by a different member of the team.

Their journey together as a team had started and quickly moved into Storming. When breakdowns occurred in the projects, the leader reverted to type and started to blame others – first the project champion, then everyone else, then me. At a two-day team workshop, the rest of the team then split into two camps which had a go at each other, and then joined up to have a go at me. I asked each of them to say what they were feeling honestly, to express how it felt to be in the team.

One person quietly and bravely expressed their feelings, only to have these flattened by a colleague who forcefully said that they felt completely different.

A third colleague then had a go at the second colleague for flattening the first, whereupon the second, more forceful colleague had a go at the third, leaving the first completely isolated. And back into Punch and Judy chaos we went.

Eventually it went quiet and I asked them to each go away and think about what they really need to say and to whom, in order to clear up or complete what had not been said or discussed. We then arranged for these one-to-ones to happen, subsequently meeting back as a team a few hours later.

The atmosphere was transformed. Unprompted by me, the group spontaneously began to talk about how they felt, what was stopping them from expressing themselves, and how they now realised how their behaviour had affected their colleagues in the past. A new level of appreciation emerged and with it, a deeper level of mutual understanding as they began to really listen to each other.

We then began to tackle some of the issues and breakdowns previously identified but with a far greater ease, mutual understanding, sense of purpose and comradeship than before.

The result was a major shift in team performance and the beginning of a new way of working.

Uses

This can be a useful way to demonstrate graphically the degree of involvement around the table. It may throw up some surprises, such as someone who seems to be contributing may feel that they are cut off or not being taken seriously. The team can then decide where they want to get to and how they believe they will achieve this. Agree the resulting actions and intentions and refer back to them at intervals. The scores can be kept to form a progress chart, or to highlight where the team needs to do further work around team communication, sharing and so on.

Any team member can use this as a shorthand checkpoint at any time that they have concerns about how the team is performing:

● where are we now?
● are we getting towards 7–8?
● how can I support John in helping him move his score around enjoyment at team meetings, and so on?

Aligning team purpose

There is usually a big alignment gap between what the team's declared purpose is and the observable behaviours in the team. This is usually because the purpose is unclear to one or more team members, and due to individuals' need to assert their individuality before cooperative alignment – hence chaos! The team coach might observe the team in action for a while, then ask themselves the following questions.

● What is the declared purpose of this team?
● Observing behaviours, what is the actual purpose?
● What is the gap between the declared and actual purpose and how is this apparent in the team's activities?
● How clear and communicated is the declared purpose?
● What are the success criteria for the team?
● Are team and individual objectives and accountabilities clearly defined and unambiguous? Are they measurable?
● What is the level of individual commitment to achieve the team goal?
● What are the issues that, if addressed, would increase commitment?

Together with the information gathered from team players individually, the coach should have an emerging picture of the team dynamic and its operating context, providing the starting point for team coaching. The general shape of the process as it continues is as follows:

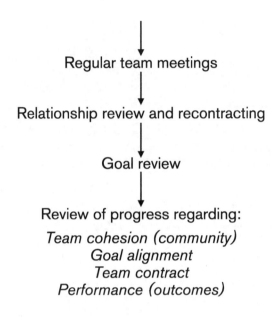

Regular team meetings

Relationship review and recontracting

Goal review

Review of progress regarding:

Team cohesion (community)
Goal alignment
Team contract
Performance (outcomes)

Indicators of success

There is nothing more difficult to carry out, nor more doubtful of success, nor more dangerous to handle, than to institute a new order of things. — Niccolò Machiavelli

Life was a bit rougher in Machiavelli's day, although I suspect many senior managers and change agents would agree with the sentiment he expresses. People assume that what has got them to the point they are now will serve them into the future. From about the age of four or five, we tend to approach life with a kind of inertia, and nowhere is this more apparent than in organisations where a 'change programme' is being introduced.

The intent behind any change programme is to improve organisational performance, and mostly this involves a departure from the mechanistic 'cog-in-the-wheel' mindset to one which embraces a free flow of information, decision-making at the lowest appropriate level and mindful risk-taking. This involves people becoming more self-reliant, more responsible and more prepared to take calculated risks where they have not done so before. This is even harder in hitherto successful organisations which superficially might look pretty safe and successful into the future. In large organisations, one warning sign is when a key division or function is particularly successful while others lag behind, when you hear variations of 'it's not our problem, the hole is at the other end of the ship'.

The landscape is always emerging and the only way to minimise risk is to maximise organisational adaptability and its capacity to flex with new conditions. Success indicators for adaptability and flex capacity might be represented through a significant shift in behaviours such as the following:

25

From:	Towards:
Risk averse	Experimental
Rank/status	Informal and relational
Rules and procedures	Flexibility and trust
Copies of emails/protect your back	Spontaneous and supportive
Failures as problems	Failures as opportunities
Rigid organisational lines	Much informal crossing
High anxiety and fear	High energy and enjoyment
Feedback as criticism	Feedback as learning
Decisions at high level	Decisions as low down as possible
Chains of command	Individual responsibility
Organisational opacity	Organisational transparency

This is of course a significant culture shift for many organisations and many managers have a great deal of themselves invested in the past, so work is always needed to be done to help facilitate the transition. My own experience as a coach is that people are very good at espousing change, but manage to undermine the process from fear of what it might mean to them.

1.4 COACHING AND MENTORING

How does coaching differ from mentoring? In a sense, there is very little to distinguish the two, as they are both about individual growth and development. Mentoring is focused primarily on the *context* of work, while coaching is focused primarily on the *content* of work, and clearly there is considerable overlap. A mentor is generally considered to be someone who 'knows the ropes', and is often older and more experienced then the mentee, both in terms of the job and in appreciating how the organisation (or, if an external mentor, the sector, e.g. law, banking, and so on) works in practice. Often they are chosen for their expertise, knowledge and perceived wisdom, which can be passed on to the mentee to improve their overall performance and self-development in their career progression in the longer term context. Coaches, or the manager-coach, focus on shorter-term, specific goals or targets that deliver measurable improvements to individual and organisational performance.

	Mentoring (context)	Coaching (content)
Skills	Listening/questioning Rapport building Challenge	Listening/questioning Rapport building Challenge
Relationship	Always one-to-one Never the line manager Either internal or external	One-to-one or team Usually the line manager Can be external
Duration	Longer term Less urgent	Shorter term More urgent
Context	Longer-term development	Shorter-term performance
Content	Advice/guidance/ encouragement Tends to be more advisory	Challenge/questions/process Tends to be more question- based
Uses	Personal development Career planning/succession Knowledge sharing	Achieving specific results Improving short-term performance Unlocking creativity
Outcomes	Knowledge shared in organisation Clarity about future development	Improved performance Increased responsibility

1.5 ETHICS AND SUPERVISION OF THE MANAGER OR COACH

Recently there have been several published incidents of managers using their position as 'coach' to encourage inappropriate personal disclosure from their line reports, to delve into personal issues and to take power over the coachee for personal advantage. Of course, this is entirely inappropriate. Neither manager nor coach should ever assert power or authority over another for personal gain. Basic ethical guidelines for the manager or coach should include the following:

● to manage and/or coach with positive intent and goodwill towards the coachee and never exploit them or the situation;
● to maintain appropriate and transparent boundaries at all times;
● to work in mutual collaboration for the best interests of the organisation.

These rules allow for an appreciative and empathic dialogue which has a robust coaching edge. They also indicate that the intent of the conversation always should be clearly understood and agreed and that it is held in the context of workplace performance. To maintain the quality of these conversations and avoid any possibility of inappropriate behaviour, some form of supervision or quality control should be available for all managers who coach in the organisation.

Coaching training and supervision for managers

Effective manager-coaches are those who have a facility and skill in flexing all eight STAMINAS (see Chapter 2) and this capacity takes time and practice to develop. One-day 'sheep dip'-style coaching training is unlikely to give managers the depth of appreciation and distinctions they need to be effective. Training should consist of at least three or four days, spread over several months, to allow for workplace practice, with review in the subsequent workshop.

Coaching is basically learned from experience, so rather than spend a lot of time (and money) doing more training, for the majority of managers subsequent development should be through action learning or supervision groups, which encourage sharing of and reflection on day-to-day practice and the development of personal action plans to maintain coaching quality. There should be a few managers who are trained to a higher level – perhaps to formal certification or coaching qualification standard – who become the 'champions' of coaching in the management line. These individuals should have coaching development as part of their job description, in order to allow them the time to support other line managers in their coaching work and to run coaching supervision groups where appropriate.

Supervision (shadow coaching)

Unfortunately, even in organisations which espouse coaching as part of management practice, there is very little in the way of ongoing support or continuous development for managers after initial coaching training. Those managers who have coaching as part of their role (and that is all of them) should be part of a larger organisational conversation around self-improvement, development and organisational learning from their coaching as well as management practice. In my experience, this varies considerably:

- their experience of coaching is not considered at all;
- it is considered, but only as a brief aside in management conversations;
- it is discussed in small specialist groups of interested managers, but best practice remains confined to the group;
- coaching practice is discussed both with the line manager and in coaching peer groups, and best practice is shared across groups.

A model for coaching supervision/shadow coaching for managers

Supervision is a formalised process originating from the helping professions through which individuals who are using 'talking therapies' with clients receive professional guidance, usually from a more experienced practitioner in their field. While coaching is not a 'talking therapy', it does engage the coachee at a deeper and more relational level; it can offer a significant challenge to entrenched behaviours and on occasions may even create personal breakthroughs that can change people's lives for the better. In this regard, coaching does impact individuals psychologically, although it is not therapy. Therefore, attention needs to be paid to ensuring that coaching remains firmly based in the context of work and does not delve into deep personal or emotional issues. Moreover, much occurs in a dialogue that is unconscious, as our own needs, prejudices, expectations and emotions permeate our listening and shape our responses out of our awareness. This makes us less effective coaches and can lead us to inadvertently collude, defer or take control of the coachee in some way.

For these reasons, supervision is essential. It should focus on what Brigid Proctor suggests are three main areas:
- *normative* – which has a focus on ethical behaviour, standards and moral and legal integrity;
- *formative* – which has a focus on learning and development;
- *restorative* – which has a focus on support and personal resilience.

Line managers who coach should have no less rigour and support of a supervisory process than practising professional coaches. To distinguish this kind of supervision in the line from other uses of the word supervision, I call this activity *shadow coaching*. A manager who is coaching-qualified at a higher level could run shadow coaching sets as part of their role accountabilities – these would be the 'champions' of coaching in the organisation. This would not be a 'bolt-on' activity, but a core part of their working week for which time is allowed, targets agreed and specific outcomes evaluated. These sets should happen every six to eight weeks or so and last perhaps two to three hours, and the managers should have additional training in coaching supervision and facilitating groups. The focus of the sets should be on helping the managers in the shadow coaching set to learn from their management and coaching experience in the line and how they could be even more effective in raising performance and learning in their respective teams. The shadow coach running the set will have in mind Proctor's trilogy, mentioned above. In addition, the conversation would include discussion of how to sustain momentum of the generic coaching conversation across the organisation in all five directions (i.e. five-way coaching – see page 8).

A further development would be the use of external coaching supervisors to facilitate and supervise or shadow coach groups of 'champions' to maximise their learning and keep them alert in their own shadow coaching. One coaching champion should be ultimately accountable for the whole process, and be regarded as the head of the community of practice (see figure overleaf).

In many organisations, this function is performed through the Human Resources function, although it could sit more appropriately within operational, client-facing functions such as sales, marketing, customer service, client operations and so on.

Head of Coaching Community of Practice

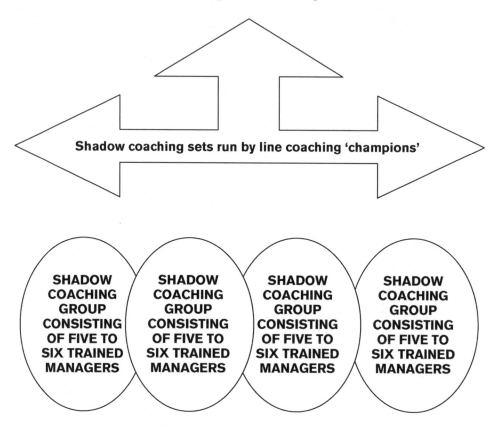

Shadow coaching sets run by line coaching 'champions'

SHADOW COACHING GROUP CONSISTING OF FIVE TO SIX TRAINED MANAGERS

SHADOW COACHING GROUP CONSISTING OF FIVE TO SIX TRAINED MANAGERS

SHADOW COACHING GROUP CONSISTING OF FIVE TO SIX TRAINED MANAGERS

SHADOW COACHING GROUP CONSISTING OF FIVE TO SIX TRAINED MANAGERS

Whoever performs the function, the individual should be a senior or board-level manager – one who is seen as a highly hands-on, practising manager demonstrating coaching best practice daily, through making every conversation they have at work an opportunity for appreciation, learning and action.

2 Fitness as a coach: the eight STAMINAS

It is clear that those people who are more skilled in the art of coaching do get better results from the people they work with – this is obvious in the sporting world, and there is increasing hard evidence in the business world. In the UK, recent Chartered Institute of Personnel and Development (CIPD) research showed that 84% of respondees to its questionnaire regarded coaching by managers to be effective. This is supported by international research freely available on the internet, as well as much anecdotal evidence.

So, if coaching really does have an impact on performance, it would seem obvious that all organisations should embrace the concept of workplace coaching. The difficulty is that for many managers, the capabilities of the effective manager or coach may require a significant shift not only in their behaviours and attitude, but also in their belief set. There are managers out there who really do think that coaching will waste valuable telling and instruction time, create a culture of decision by committee and dilute their managerial authority – all of which is erroneous. Coaching facilitates deeper understanding and responsibility, reducing the time required for instruction and allowing for appropriate decision-making further away from the manager, freeing up even more of their time. As for diluting their managerial authority, there is a common misunderstanding that managerial authority is the same as managerial control. It is not – managers do not have to give up their authority, but they do have to relinquish the need to control other people. This shift in mindset is crucial if coaching is to be fully espoused in organisations.

The capabilities needed to coach effectively require managers to consider not only their behaviours and attitudes, but to inquire more deeply into their personal values and beliefs about the meaning of work, the potential of others to perform outstandingly, and their own blocks to learning and development which are almost certainly making them less effective as managers than they could be.

There are eight key areas of capability that the effective manager or coach will display: the coaching STAMINAS, which is an acronym for:

- Structuring
- Toughness
- Affinity
- Mobility
- Intuition
- Norms
- Action-orientation
- Support.

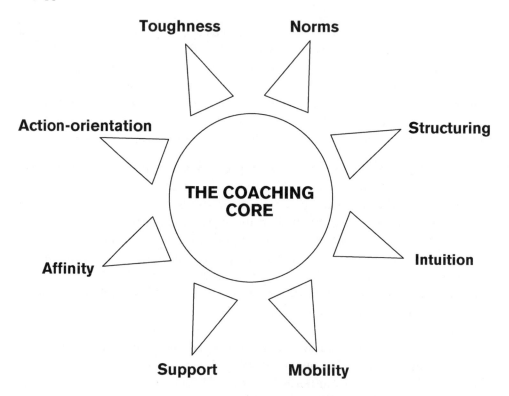

The STAMINAS are paired, with each of the four pairs having a particular coaching orientation:

- Intuition and Mobility have a *creative* coaching orientation;
- Toughness and Action-orientation have a *offensive* coaching orientation (offensive as in pushing forward and directed at scoring);
- Support and Affinity have a *relational* coaching orientation; and
- Norms and Structuring have an *empirical* coaching orientation.

These four orientations – creative, offensive, relational and empirical – are described more fully in Chapter 3, where the STAMINAS questionnaire will guide you towards your preferred coaching orientation. The following section describes each of the eight STAMINAS in more detail.

2.1 Number One – **STRUCTURING**

Real conversation catches fire. It involves more than sending or receiving information. Conversation does not simply reshuffle the pack. It creates new cards. — Theodore Zeldin

Coaching conversations are different from our normal experience of conversation. They are focused on achieving a specific result, and it is this focus which helps to create the conditions for awareness and learning. Also, a coach ensures that coaching conversations are structured in terms of the process, not the content – that is always driven by the coachee. *Structure in coaching conversations should always be rigorous but never rigid.*

A coaching conversation has a specific structure which allows both coach and coachee to examine the performer's understanding of an issue or problem, to see it in its true entirety and to take action to change or improve it. Here is an analogy from my own experience:

I was about 10, at school and working out the quickest and safest way of walking from A to B by learning how to read an Ordnance Survey map, which I found very confusing. I knew the lines on the map translated into a landscape, but somehow I could not picture it. It made no sense and the more I tried to work it out, the more rivers ran uphill, roads disappeared and mountains became valleys.

Now it just so happened that the (very patient) geography teacher who was teaching me to map-read had an accurate plasticine three-dimensional model of the same landscape created from the same map. Once I saw the model, it all became clear.

Looking at the map was creating assumptions and pictures in my head which weren't true (and in some cases impossible), and seeing the whole thing in 3D was revelatory. It was now obvious to me which route I should take to reach my goal – all I needed was to have a different perspective.

Structure allows the conversation to have a shape, purpose and direction. It is the crucible in which the conversation occurs and defines its limits and parameters. Without structure, the conversation can fall apart quickly into an unfocused dialogue which may have merit in itself – the open listening afforded by the coach is powerful in its own right – but which will not necessarily give the coachee a clear focus for commitment to action.

Effective coaches structure their coaching conversations with rigour and skill. They ensure that the conversation has a clear goal, engage the coachee by asking probing but non-leading questions, and follow a set and proven pattern which finishes with clarity about next steps and commitment to action. The structure most commonly used by coaches is the To GROW model.

The To GROW model

The To GROW model is a well-established coaching model and probably the most widely used for structuring a performance coaching conversation. (First proposed by Graham Alexander, John Whitmore is widely acknowledged as the coach who has popularised this model internationally, and his book *Coaching for Performance* is one of the industry's all-time bestsellers.)

This five-stage model starts with phase 1, which is a conversation about the coachee's *Topic*, followed by phase 2, *Goal* (for the session). Phase 3 is a conversation to deepen mutual understanding around the coachee's current *Reality*, phase 4 is *Options*, and phase 5 is *Will* or *Way forward* (occasionally referred to as *Wrap-up*, although this has less indication of movement and action).

In fact, the conversation will hardly ever be linear and will slide seamlessly from phase to phase and back again a number of times during the conversation. The role of the coach is to understand where they are in the model and to ensure that all the phases are discussed.

The To GROW model

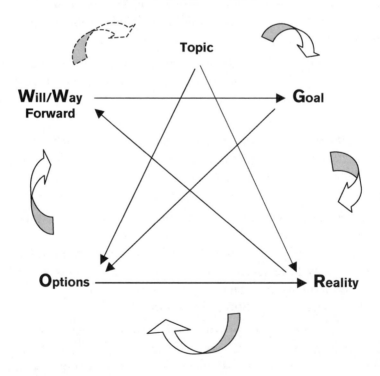

Purpose of each phase
- *Topic* – to understand the coachee's general issue (context, scale, emotional attachment, longer-term goal) and to contextualise the conversation;
- *Goal* – what does the coachee want to achieve from *this* conversation? What would success look or sound like? Have a final destination for the conversation: this is not about long-term goals, just the outcome of the current conversation;
- *Reality* – deepening mutual understanding about the issue, raising awareness, examining assumptions and self-limiting beliefs, gaining deeper clarity and insight, understanding practical limitations and appreciating paradox;
- *Options* – what are all the possible options for action? Challenge assumptions and negativity and push the coachee to think wide and creatively: what else could they do? What will be most effective? What would be crazy but fun (within boundaries)?
- *Will/Way forward* – what is the coachee going to do and by when? What is the intended outcome and how will they know that it has worked? Check alignment of actions with the original goal: what help do they need and where will they get it? What is their commitment now, on a scale of 1 to 10, for taking action – if not 10, how could it be so? Provide support and discuss the next meeting.

With practice and experience, the coach will acquire an ease with structuring conversations in this way such that, whatever conversational structure they are following, it will recede into the background of their awareness. Those less practised often say that the models get in the way of their listening for the coachee and become more of a hindrance than a help. It really is worth persevering – without the background structure, a coaching conversation will soon turn into an aimless chat with lack of focus, poor concentration and unclear outcomes.

Almost invariably when discussing their *Topic*, coachees will begin to explain their current situation in more depth, moving to some degree straight into the *Reality* phase of the conversation. The coachee may even come up with an option or two at this stage. At some point the coach should move the conversation back to *Goal* for the session, then back into *Reality* and explore further options. Specific actions may be agreed throughout the conversation, not only at the end – although a final summary and commitment to action is important.

Questions around Topic
Every conversation needs to start somewhere, preferably at the beginning! The purpose of the *Topic* phase of the GROW model is to get a brief overview of the performer's situation as they see it now and set the scene for the coaching conversation that follows. The coach initiates the conversation by asking the

coachee to explain briefly the situation in which they find themselves. They will describe some kind of breakdown which has stopped them in action and it will be around themselves, their relationships with others, an external or environmental factor or a combination of some or all of these. Typically, you might hear one or more of the following.

Topics around themselves as individuals:
- lack of skill;
- lack of knowledge;
- low self-esteem or confidence;
- negative attitude;
- low energy;
- lack of clarity around purpose or goal;
- stress issues;
- personal motivation;
- the 'dog choker' effect (self-doubt, fear or embarrassment that is holding them back from doing something that they want or need to do).

Topics around relationships with others:
- communication with individuals or team;
- motivating others;
- negotiating win–win with others;
- failed attempts to modify others' behaviours;
- resentment, anger or frustration with lack of action;
- building relationships;
- lack of agreement or alignment;
- missing conversations around goals or objectives;
- team issues.

Topics around external or environmental factors:
- difficult trading conditions;
- economic recession;
- high or 'stretch' targets (see p. 70);
- a declining market for services or products;
- organisational IT or communication technology not effective;
- procedures or processes inappropriate or ineffective;
- lack of time or resources;
- issues around structure.

As coach, your role is simply to listen to the topic and to be clear that you understand it. This will require you to *summarise* once you think you have understood. Once you and the coachee are clear about the topic, move the conversation on, using the coachee's interest to guide you.

Questions around Goal

The purpose of effective coaching is to create a thinking space for the coachee to explore their issue or problem from an objective viewpoint, and in the process to surface entrenched assumptions. This kind of thinking requires a focus, so effective coaching conversations always have a clear goal.

One reason why a coaching conversation can seem circular and ineffective is that there is a lack of clarity around the goal for the conversation. There must be a goal, even if the goal is to get really clear about the goal! Also, it is important to understand that an agreed aspirational end goal – say, to treble turnover in the next six months, or to deliver a challenging project on time and under budget – will be broken down into smaller performance goals, and it is these 'bitesize chunks' that form the basis for day-to-day coaching conversation goals. For example:

Aspirational end goal:
● to win 20% more customers in the next 12 months in a contracting market.

Performance goals:
● to create more effective teamworking across the organisation;
● to develop a new IT system to capture customer or market information;
● to develop my communication and leadership skills.

Each of these performance goals will involve the coachee taking specific actions as they commit to moving forwards. The coaching focuses on the action and the subsequent learning, leading to further goals, action and more learning. This iterative process increases rapidly in speed as the coachee gathers momentum. The coach is there to focus this momentum towards achieving the coachee's aspirational goal in the agreed timescale.

For example, the coachee may say that their *topic* is about a problem that they are having with their boss at work: in the conversation, the issue becomes clear that the coachee feels pressurised and unable to say no to his boss, causing them stress and lack of confidence. The *goal* for the conversation may focus on some actions that the coachee can take in relation to this issue. They then describe an *invented future* in which their relationship to their boss is stronger and more equal, where 'no' is easier to say, and in which the coachee is regularly coping successfully with large amounts of work.

Success measures might be discussed and include, for example, having regular meetings with the boss, declining one particular piece of work, finishing a major project within three months and some behavioural indicators that demonstrate better communication and understanding between the performer and their boss. The coachee now has a number of choices about where to focus, to use the conversation to improve their performance. For example, they might choose to think of ways to finish the project more quickly, or how to engage their boss in more regular meetings, or to examine how they might think differently about saying 'no' more often. One or possibly more of these choices now become the focus of the conversation and specific related actions are the intended outcome.

Before moving on, the coach needs to be sure that the intended outcome is congruent – that is, will the coachee leave the conversation with some learning and action that will mobilise them towards their longer term goal? Also, is the outcome realistic within the timeframe of the conversation? 'I want to have some ideas about how to tackle the chronic absenteeism in my department' is probably a perfectly appropriate outcome to aim for in a half-hour coaching conversation. However, 'I want to define my personal values in relation to this organisation and its values' is a longer-term goal which would need to be teased apart into smaller components, in order to discover the most appropriate and achievable outcome for the session.

CASE STUDY

When I was younger, I was a junior instructor at a karate club. One evening after training the younger of two brothers, who were club members, came up to me in the *dojo* and asked for some extra training so he 'could kick higher'. I remember the two brothers were nicknamed 'Little and Large' – the younger brother Paul being so much shorter than his older brother, Josh.

I assumed that Paul's intention was to increase his kick range by a couple of inches. Paul and I spent a good hour stretching and sparring in the *dojo*, focusing on the *mawashigeri* roundhouse kick. By the end of a hard evening, Paul was definitely able to extend his kick further, yet seemed dissatisfied with this outcome, which I thought was pretty good. I then asked the question that I should have asked at the beginning:

'Paul, exactly what did you want to have achieved by the end of this session?' He replied: 'I want to kick higher than my brother.'

Paul would have needed major orthopaedic surgery over several years to even think about kicking higher than his taller brother. Because of a lack of mutual clarity and assumption on my part about expected outcome, Paul was dispirited and upset, despite his measurable performance increase.

Paul went on to become one of the club's finest exponents of *kata*, which requires perfection of technique rather than physical size.

- How will you tell that you are reaching your goal?
- What will begin to change as you move towards your goal?

- What will success sound/look/feel like?
- What timeframe will you set for achieving your goal and what do you want to have happened by the end of the first week/month, the second week/month, and so on?
- What changes will you see in other people's behaviour or attitudes, and in what timeframe?
- Who will give you feedback about your successes, how do you want them to give it and how often?
- If you noticed only one thing changing, what would that be? How would you know it was changing?

Questions around Reality

- On a scale of 1 to 10, where are you now and what upward shift in the scale would indicate success to you?
- Tell me more about the situation?
- What's your level of commitment to moving forward?
- Who is involved?
- What have you done so far?
- Who have you spoken to or got involved?
- What effect did that have?
- How much authority do you have around this issue?
- What has stopped you so far in resolving this?
- What might stop you taking action now?
- What, if anything, is stopping others acting to resolve this with you?
- What do you think is going on – for you, for other people?
- What do you feel about the situation?
- What do you think others are feeling or wanting?

Questions around *Reality* can be given in general by:

- asking open questions – who, how, what, when;
- exploring the use of language such as metaphors, repeated words;
- accurately reflecting language and summarising;
- giving feedback:
  - informal – 'I notice that you ...'
  - prepared – such as a 360° questionnaire, where the individual receives anonymised formal feedback from others who know the individual in a variety of work situations
  - inductive – 'What impact do you think your action had?'
- challenging and exploring assumptions;
- encouraging personal reflection;
- encouraging explanation of the wider context;

- challenging self-limiting beliefs:
  - 'If you knew you could...'
  - 'If there were time or money...', and so on.

Questions around Options
- What else could you do other than those things we have already discussed?
  - ...and what else?
  - ...and what else?
  - ...and what else?
- If you had all the resources you needed, what would you do?
- If you had a magic wand, what would you do?
- If you knew you were unstoppable, what is the first thing you would do?
- If it were entirely within your authority, what changes would you make?
- If you knew that people's reaction would be to agree with you 100%, what actions would you recommend?
- If you knew you could not fail, what would you do?
- What's the one thing you haven't tried yet because you thought it was too outrageous/bizarre/funny?
- What would your best friend/worst enemy/business adviser/mum/dad advise you to do?

Questions around Will/Way forward
- What are you going to do now/first?
- What is the timeframe?
- What are the milestones towards success?
- What support, if any, can I offer you?
- What might stop you in action?
- What downside if any do you see around this action/these actions?
- What is the intended outcome of this action/these actions?
- Will this action achieve your goal? How will you know?
- How will that move you nearer your goal?
- What might stop you in action?
- If there are any downsides identified, what could you do to reduce or minimise these?
- What's your commitment (on a scale of 1 to 10)?
- What's missing that has you score your commitment level under 9?
- How could you move your commitment nearer 10?
- How could you adjust your identified actions that would have your commitment to action nearer 10?
- What's holding you back from action?
- What conversations do you need to have, when and with whom, in order to achieve your desired outcome?

The purpose of this part of the To GROW model is to create energy and commitment to action. If there is no commitment to some kind of specific action, then you have had a pleasant chat – which in itself has relational value and may be very helpful (sometimes it is what the coachee needs) – but generally, action is the name of the game. The action does not necessarily have to be physical – it might be, for example, to reflect on a particular situation and work out how to be more effective next time that it happens – although any action as a result of coaching should be noted and reviewed. Most actions as a result of coaching will involve the coachee in doing something different, approaching someone they have not spoken to but need to speak to, addressing a specific task with more resolution and energy and generally being more 'in action'.

Beware of letting the coachee 'off the hook' by accepting a reduced commitment to action – just because they are going to find this action tough or difficult does not mean that they shouldn't do it! If your sense of the coachee is that they are playing a small game, encourage them to consider what could be available to them by being more bold or authoritative. It is the coach's job to help the coachee raise their own performance bar and not to collude with them in keeping it low.

Ensure you are both crystal clear on what is going to happen next, offer your support if appropriate, and agree a time for review (particularly if you are the line manager).

Closing the coaching session

A coaching conversation is one that builds the relationship, so it is particularly important to leave the conversation with a sense of closure. An effective way of doing this is for the coach to ask for feedback from the coachee at the end of the session. A question I ask often is:

What do you want to say about the way we have worked together today?

The intent behind this is to elicit some genuine feedback that I can use subsequently to build my relationship with the coachee and to make my coaching more effective for them next time we meet. The question is very open and makes the assumption that there *is* something to say – because there always is! More specific questions to elicit feedback might include the following.

- On a scale of 1 to 10, how well did this session meet your expectations in terms of expected outcome/non-directive coaching/my attention/challenge?
- How could we make these sessions even more effective for you?
- What could I do to be more effective for you as a coach?

- What could we do more of/less of to make these sessions more effective for you?
- Is there anything you would like to say to complete this session today?

Although simple, it takes time and practice to become fluent with the To GROW model, in much the same way as learning to drive a car. Practice is essential – fortunately, the workplace provides almost limitless opportunities to practise structuring conversations to improve performance.

2.2   Number Two – **TOUGHNESS**

You have probably heard the expressions 'tough love' or 'ruthless compassion'. They mean the same thing: caring enough for someone and for their commitment to achieve that you are prepared to make it hot in the kitchen for you both (be clear – if you are not finding it tough too, then you are not appreciating how hard it is for them).

Challenging

A key role of the coach is to challenge the coachee's thinking, negative mindset, self-limiting beliefs and ineffective behaviours that produce poor results or have detrimental impact on relationships. When the coach hears 'downward spiral' talk (this is too hard/it's not for me/I can't do this/just tell me how to do it, and so on), explanations and excuses, it is time to challenge the individual – on what basis are they making such assertions? What is the evidence?

If you offer a challenge, do make sure that the support you offer is clear, unambiguous and sufficient to cover the challenge you have set for the coachee. The best performance emerges in the high challenge/high support category:

- *low challenge/low support* – low energy, resentment, boredom; (typically, the management style is *laissez-faire*, lacking clarity of direction or objectives);
- *low challenge/high support* – comfort, moderate energy, disengaged; (typically, the management style is collusive, conflict-averse and lacks rigour);
- *high challenge/low support* – high energy, anxiety, stressed; (typically, the management style is aggressive, unempathic, results-driven and egocentric);
- *high challenge/high support* – very high energy, calm, engaged; (typically, the management style is appreciative, rigorous and performance-focused).

Here we make a distinction between *results-driven* and *performance-focused*. On the one hand, striving for results may not give better performance (although it will raise anxiety in the performer); striving for performance always gives better results. Of course, goals and objectives must be in place and should be clear and measurable within a timeframe. On the other hand, over-concern about achieving goals will lead to anxiety, doubt, nervousness, and so on, and this will detract from performance – just when it is needed most.

Great performers, whoever they are, want to 'win' – but on the field of play (whatever kind of field that happens to be), their focus is on *playing their best game right here and now*, not specifically on winning the game in the near future. (More on this approach to performance can be found in Tim Gallwey's 'Inner Game' approach to coaching, which created a fundamental and permanent shift in coaching style from the 1970s onwards).

> *When the archer shoots for no particular prize, he has all his skills. When he shoots to win a brass buckle, he is already nervous; when he shoots for a gold prize, he goes blind – he sees two targets and is out of his mind. His skill has not changed but the prize divides him. He cares! He thinks more of winning than of shooting and the need to win drains him of power.*
>
> — Tranxu, Chinese sage

The message here is that the best performance is achieved through relaxed and focused attention to the task in hand, and this in turn is achieved through supportive and structured coaching conversations. Don't expect the coachee to always be in high challenge/high support – occasionally they will need a rest, a period to recharge batteries, so low challenge/high support would be entirely appropriate in this case.

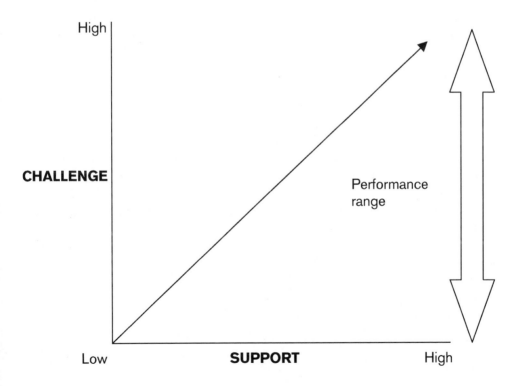

Examples of coaching challenges might include the following:

- I'd like to challenge you on that/what you said just now...
- My sense is that you have given up/are not committed to this project...
- You and I clearly contracted for X and you haven't done what you said you'd do. Tell me what happened?
- I don't believe this piece of work is beyond your ability...
- You are playing a small game which is I believe below your potential...
- Don't blame this issue on others.../You must take responsibility yourself...
- I know you can raise the stakes here...
- If you knew you could succeed, what would you do/say...

Giving feedback

All living things are feedback systems. From the lowliest blob of pond life to a human being, all living things get feedback from their environment moment by moment and use that information instantaneously to carry on living and moving as effectively as possible.

The purpose of feedback is to help a person or a team understand the impact of their actions and behaviours, and help them to become more effective. The intention is to raise the other person's awareness, so they understand and appreciate how they are being experienced. The process gives them information that allows them to alter their behaviour – if they choose. Everyone is free to choose – however, every choice has consequences and understanding the consequences will also alter behaviour.

Feedback is most effective when the recipient has given permission for it to take place: 'How did I do? How am I doing?' They are then in a receptive frame of mind, are likely to think about the information and discuss how performance can be improved. At work, it is sometimes the leader's role to give feedback, even where it might not be welcome: 'We need to talk about how you are getting on.' This means creating the permission oneself. If the intention is to be helpful it will not be seen as confrontational, although it may be uncomfortable. Either way, there needs to be permission or a contract to give feedback. This may be implicit in the line manager or coach's role, but the process needs to be clear and unambiguous to be most effective. If you anticipate that the discussion will be a battle from the outset, try asking yourself what the overall goal is and how you can explain it in a way that the other person is likely to be able to hear and understand. Put yourself in the other person's shoes and try thinking through the conversation from their perspective. This will usually suggest ways of approaching the topic that reduce the likelihood of conflict, for example: 'How do you think you have been doing?' 'How are you finding working with this team?'

Be specific

Generalisations are not useful feedback. 'That was a terrible presentation' does not help the presenter to identify what went wrong and decide on the improvements necessary. It is very important to refer to particular words or actions, to help the recipient to remember what they said or did – that is, their behaviours. For example, 'Your slides were crowded, so I could not follow the diagrams' is helpful feedback, as it provides specific information and points to improvement actions.

When giving feedback:

- Get or create permission to give feedback
- Ask the individual to assess their own performance first
- Be clear for whose benefit it is
- Get your time and place right
- Say why you are giving this feedback
- Be very specific, use facts and examples
- Focus on 'do-able' changes
- Balance positives and negatives
- Focus on behaviour, not personality

When receiving feedback:

- Listen with an open mind
- Notice what you did and the impact it had on the situation or people
- Try not to be defensive
- Don't interrupt or justify
- Try to appreciate it as a gift
- Accept the feedback and clarify as necessary
- Say thanks – it may have been as hard to give as it was to receive
- Remember that feedback is only one opinion
- Act on the feedback if you believe it will make a difference

(Reproduced from *Leadership 101* with kind permission of Margaret Lloyd and Brian Rothwell)

Balance positive and negative

Begin positively, so that they know what they are doing well. Effective feedback must contain the negative, so that the person knows what needs to improve. Be honest about whether this is your personal opinion: 'I liked the way you involved the whole team', or a difficulty affecting several people: 'I have had several complaints about the pictures used in the posters for this campaign because of X and Y.'

Check it out

It is important to focus on 'do-able' changes and to check that the recipient has understood the feedback given. Always check out of the conversation with a short discussion about how it could be better next time. Focus on observed behaviours and create the feedback as data. Be specific about the time, place and situation that you are referring to and state what you *noticed* (saw, heard or felt) about the person to whom you are giving feedback. Clearly state what you noticed as the consequence of their action, then discuss the feedback as constructive data to inform future behaviour.

CASE STUDIES

Case study 1

At the end of a team coaching session, I asked the question of the group: 'Have you anything you want to say about how we have worked together today?' The team members were complimentary about each other's contribution and had nothing but positive things to say about me, the coach. This was very nice of them, but totally unhelpful in terms of my learning how I could be more effective next time as coach for them.

I gave them this feedback, which was a reflection of the way they had been working with each other and asked them to be honest with me. I elicited some valuable feedback about visibility of flipcharts, timing of breaks and a ground rule which I had not enforced. (I also got less helpful feedback about my tie – long story!) The lesson is: always elicit feedback – whether you use it or not is up to you.

Case study 2

I was coaching a senior executive in a financial consultancy. It was the end of our third session and I asked what she would like to say about the way we had worked together during the session. She told me that she felt it had been particularly useful to focus on an issue which had only emerged through a throwaway comment of hers at the beginning of the session. She also found the rigour of the action planning gave her real clarity of action. I acknowledged this.

'Anything else?' I asked.

'Yes,' she replied. 'I felt at one point in the conversation you were leading me to adopt your own point of view.' And she explained why she thought this. As she did so and I asked a question or two for clarification, I realised that in one key area of action, I had indeed been running my own agenda.

The lesson for me was that of transparency – if, as a coach, I really need to say something because it is in my head (so preventing me from being completely attentive to the coachee), then I need to say it, not manipulate the coachee towards it. How easily we fall into this trap.

2.3   Number Three – **AFFINITY**

We are all very attached to who we think we are – it is our ground of being, our story of our life, our beliefs in what we think is possible and not possible and what has brought us more or less successfully to where we are now in our individual lives.

The concept of the person as a self-authored story allows for several possibilities. First, it means that my personal story (me, my life, the way I feel and think about the world – my perceptions) is like any other story: it can be reinterpreted, rewritten or completely authored anew. It means that potentially, others 'reading' my story can get something completely different from me. It also indicates that as author, I have absolute control over the story, and therefore responsibility over what I create as being 'me'. So, in order for me to understand and appreciate another person fully, I have to listen to their 'story' without judgement or opinion. In a coaching relationship between two people, there are actually three entities: the coach, the coachee and the relationship between them.

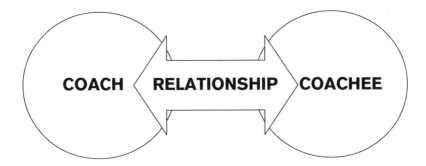

The relationship between coach and coachee has an existence of its own. An effective coach will be aware of what they are thinking and feeling themselves (i.e. their story), what the coachee might be thinking and feeling (i.e. the coachee's story) and how both of these separate viewpoints are being played out in the relationship between them. We sometimes call this *the relational space* – a space which can be opened up or closed down, according to the capability of the coach and the quality of the relationship.

We cannot help but bring our thoughts and feelings into this space. However, we can reduce the impact of any negative dynamics by being aware of how we are being affected by the coachee and how we might be affecting them. This self-awareness on the part of the coach helps to open up the relational space and leads to authentic affinity.

Affinity starts with listening (whether aural or by interpreting signs). Our consciousness, the way the world appears to us, our feelings, the meaning that we give to those feelings and our reactions – everything that makes us who we are and what we do is created in our *listening*. Listening is the ground of individual being on which we each stand. I stand in my ground, you stand in yours, and so on for every person on the planet. If you cannot listen to another person and understand the world that they inhabit, you can have no real affinity for them. I am not you and my ground is not yours. This means we each listen to the world differently. We don't just have a point of view, we *are* a point of view. In fact, we are *the* point of view: we expect and profoundly believe that everyone else sees the same world as we do. This makes us all designed to be judgemental and opinionated from our worldview. It is just the way we are.

> *The self is not a thing but a point of view which unifies the flow of experience into a coherent narrative, a narrative striving to connect with other narratives and become richer.*
> — Jerome Bruner, 'Research Currents', *Language Arts*, pp. 574–83

Successful people understand the importance and benefits of stepping beyond their own ground and to 'get' the world as another 'gets' it – this is listening without judgement, limit, prejudice, opinion or values. When you appreciate how someone else really 'is' – as opposed to your own view of how you think they are – then the relationship changes. It becomes deeper, more trusting, more related. It is in relationships that successful people generate and sustain their success. No one ever succeeded at anything without the help, learning, feedback and support of other people.

So, it follows that to be extraordinary, we have to be an extraordinary listener. What does this mean?

What is 'listening'?

> *What you are sounds so loudly in my ears that I can't hear what you say.*
> — Ralph Waldo Emerson

As humans, our only access to reality as we know it is through our thinking (no thoughts, no consciousness). Since we 'listen' to our thoughts, it follows that awareness of our world is also through our listening. We cannot think anything or be aware of anything until we have somehow 'listened' to it in our thinking.

In our 'listening' to the world in this way, each of us has constructed a reality or 'story' about who we are and our place in the world – how we individually fit, how we survive and what will serve us individually in order somehow to come out on top. This story is, of course, all about 'me' and gives me the sense of 'being in here' and you (and everyone and everything else) 'being out there'. However, reality isn't like that. Modern science proves reality to be very different. To quote Gary Zukav in *The Dancing Wu Li Masters*:

> *What is 'out there' apparently depends, in a rigorous mathematical sense as well as a philosophical one, upon what we decide 'in here'. (p. 115)*

As Margaret Wheatley explains in her book, *Leadership and the New Science*:

> *The new physics cogently explains that there is no objective reality out there waiting to reveal its secrets. There are no recipes, or formulae, no checklists or advice that describe 'reality'. There is only what we create through our engagement with others and with events. (p. 7)*

As you might expect, Albert Einstein also had something to say on the matter of reality:

> *A human being is part of the whole, called by us universe; a part limited by time and space. He experiences himself, his thoughts and feelings, as something separate from the rest, a kind of optical delusion of consciousness. This delusion is a kind of prison for us, restricting us to our personal desires and to affection for a few persons nearest us. Our task must be to free ourselves from this prison.*

The bottom line is that each of us has a particular and unique way of 'listening' to the world. Into this we load up with our personal views of what is right and wrong, judgements, prejudices, 'should and should nots', opinions, assumptions, reasons why things are the way things are and excuses for why they cannot be different. All of this is perfectly normal, but as Einstein points out, it is a kind of prison. It prevents us from appreciating what is possible beyond the limits of our personal worldview, and the role of the coach is to do just that – to help people see beyond their own possibility horizon.

An effective coach gets beyond their own story in order to help the coachee to see their own. Getting beyond our own story when we coach is one of the constant development issues for the coach. It is a fallacy that anyone can fully listen to another for a consistent length of time. We are simply not made that way. The best we can do is to *become more aware* of when we are not listening attentively to someone and 'wake up' to listening with full attention again. As a trainee coach once said to me:

> *I need to be aware of my listening going through the prism of my own perception.*

Distractions from listening

We have a very varied and often very low attention span, particularly if we consider the speaker boring (although 'boring' exists only in the listener). Other distractions might include:

- trying to be in control or 'on top';
- asserting or holding a personal agenda;
- worrying about being right, or getting it wrong;
- trying or wanting to help;

- having answers;
- trying to be a coach;
- looking smart;
- lacking courage;
- needing a result;
- getting attached.

To listen effectively, we have to learn how to reduce the length of time that we 'drift' from total attentiveness (the *attention frequency*) and the depth to which we have 'drifted away' (the *attention amplitude*). There is only one way of learning how to do this and that is, of course, through practice – both by doing coaching and by being coached. Listening drift occurs when we listen to ourselves: that is, when we follow our own interest, not that of the speaker. For example, make a note of your own answers to the following statements:

- I enjoy listening to people who ...
- I get bored by people who talk about ...
- I am irritated or angered by people whose stories include ...
- I feel embarrassed or upset when the conversation involves ...
- I feel inclined to interrupt or have my say when someone is talking about ...
- I want to offer advice or guidance when the other person talks about ...

Can you be aware enough of your own interests to put these to one side in order to give full attention to another person? The problem is that we allow our own preferences or interests to shape and filter what we hear, when we do make the effort to listen.

The listening space

When two people meet together for a specific purpose such as coaching, and whether we are aware of it or not, there are dynamics that are generated between the two people. These dynamics arise on both sides from:

- our preconceptions and assumptions of people:
  - the way they speak;
  - dialect or accent;
  - the way they dress;
  - body shape;
  - level of fitness;
  - skin colour;
  - nationality;
  - religion, and so on;
- our beliefs:
  - behaviours we value;
  - attitudes we think are important;

- our personal values:
  - the things we hold dear;
  - the things which drive our attitudes;
- our opinions:
  - what is good or bad;
  - what is right or wrong;
  - stereotyping.

Often these dynamics are deeply unconscious or subconscious and can help or hinder the flow of understanding, depending on the circumstances. Unconscious clashes in the dynamics between two people in the listening space can make for confusing, irritating and ineffective communication – in effect, they close the space down. Unhelpful dynamics allow only a limited listening space, while helpful dynamics create far more opportunity for listening space – a space which holds the possibility of bold thinking and committed action. So, the more we make these dynamics conscious to ourselves, the more effective we can be as listeners.

Antagonistic dynamics push against each other and reduce the listening space
In this situation – which is typical of most ordinary conversations – our personal listening filters (preconceptions, beliefs, opinions, and so on) push into the listening space and reduce the possibility of what might occur.

The dynamics generated are most influenced by our personal experiences from the past and our automatic reactions to them. For example, if in the past I was frightened by a tall person with long black hair, then it is possible that I will perceive all tall people with long black hair as potentially frightening, and on a subconscious level I will be wary of them – or at least until I have got to know them better and they have proven that they are not the stereotype in which I have cast them. Shorter people often perceive taller people as dominating, highly successful people can appear to be daunting, uniformed personnel such as police officers or customs officers can trigger fear, deference or rebelliousness. Someone might immediately remind you of a mean or kind teacher you once had, an eccentric aunt or uncle, or the school bully in primary school, triggering subconscious dynamics between you.

When I meet therapists informally in my work as a coach I sometimes notice a feeling of anxiety – Am I being analysed? What might I be revealing without knowing it? All of this can occur without our being aware of it, and yet it has a huge impact on how two or more people communicate. It gets in the way of listening openly, non-judgementally and with genuine interest.

Helpful dynamics pull with each other and increase the listening space
Being aware of how we are being impacted by the speaker, and how we might be impacting them, allows us to reduce antagonistic dynamics and focus on listening to open up the space that is created in authentic dialogue.

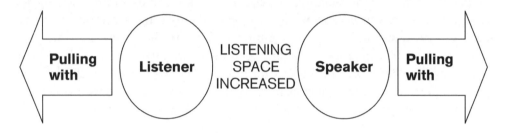

The painter Henri Matisse wrote in his 85th year:

> *The art of portraiture is one of the most remarkable. It demands especial gifts of the artist and the possibility of an almost total identification of the painter with the model. The painter should come to his model with no preconceived ideas ... Something comes into being, an interaction of feeling which makes each sense the warmth of the other's heart.* — Matisse on Art, p. 222

Awareness provides the information to help us change our actions and there are some specific areas that we can focus on, to increase our own self-awareness, that will create positive and helpful dynamics. This will help to create a more open listening space. There are three places where we can focus our attention: things we can see, what we are thinking and how we are feeling.

Awareness of interpersonal dynamics: placing attention

The more we notice what is going on for us in the moment when we are in conversation, the more effective we are in creating a listening space. We can place our attention in three main areas: our physical world (things we can observe or feel physically), our mental world (things we think) and our emotional world (what we feel emotionally).

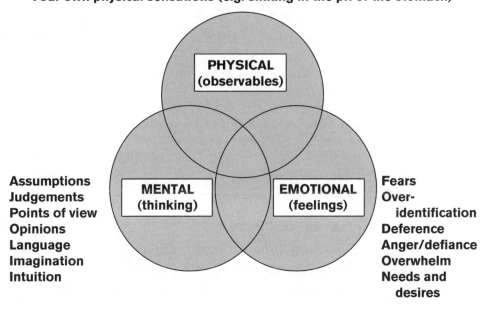

Appearance and dress
Gender
Height
How you meet
Where you meet
How you sit (both height and proximity)
Body language
Taking notes
Your own physical sensations (e.g. sinking in the pit of the stomach)

PHYSICAL (observables)

MENTAL (thinking)

EMOTIONAL (feelings)

Assumptions
Judgements
Points of view
Opinions
Language
Imagination
Intuition

Fears
Over-
   identification
Deference
Anger/defiance
Overwhelm
Needs and
   desires

One key distinction is important to make here, which is to separate out the antagonistic dynamics from the helpful dynamics. To put it another way, dump the stuff that is about you personally and use the stuff that is occurring helpfully as information in the relational space between you and the coachee. For example, you meet someone for the first time and you notice you feel a bit in awe. It would be useful to understand what this feeling of awe is about. Are they a senior person evoking in you a sense of inferiority due to something in your past? If so, put it on one side and don't let it get in the way. If you still notice the sense of awe, perhaps you are picking up a reflection (technically, this is transference) from them – maybe they are in awe of you! This could be useful information to notice. Perhaps this happens on a regular basis for the coachee, unconsciously robbing them of power in their relationships with others.

	About the listener	*About the speaker*
Physical (observables)	• Gender • Ethnicity • Age • Height • Attire • Energy • Appearance • Body language • Style Physical sensations (tingling, sinking feeling, and so on)	• Gender • Ethnicity • Age • Height • Attire • Energy • Appearance • Body language • Style
Mental (thinking and imagination)	This person reminds me of... My opinion of them as a person is... I think what they are saying is... I agree/disagree with them as... Their words/use of language is... I've heard this before when... My advice to them is... They're not very clever... They're way cleverer than me... They are junior/senior to me... This person is powerful/powerless... My fantasy about them is...	You can make a guess or create an hypothesis, or you will have to ask them.

	About the listener	About the speaker
Emotional (feelings and intuition)	The feelings this person is evoking in me are: ● angry ● sad ● happy ● tired ● bored ● irritated ● exhausted ● afraid ● overwhelmed ● attracted ● repelled ● in awe ● deferential ● in charge I want... I need... Intuitively I think/feel that...	You can make a guess or create an hypothesis, or you will have to ask them.

Effective listening creates the space for effective dialogue

Effective listening is attentive, accurate and empathetic. It is listening behind the words used by the speaker to understand what is being communicated between the words:

● What kind of words and expressions is the person using?
● What emotions or feelings are being expressed?
● What is not being said or expressed?
● What metaphors or figures of speech are being used?

What does this data tell you about the interests and needs of the speaker? From this place of mutual understanding, questions and occasionally more directive interventions will flow naturally.

Being aware of body language

Words count for less than 18% of communication. Tone of voice accounts for around 27% and at least 55% is non-verbal behaviour. So it is really important to be aware of your own body language as well as being fully aware of what the coachee's own body language is telling you.

Helpful behaviours would be those of the interested and engaged listener who is fascinated by what the other person has to say. You can imagine for yourself what this might look like, and would include:

- mirroring the coachee's body language;
- nodding appropriately;
- keeping an open, upright posture;
- maintaining eye contact but not staring;
- leaning forward but not over too much;
- showing a sense of interest and care in what the person is saying.

Obviously, yawning, being slumped in the chair, having crossed arms, looking away, shaking your head or appearing generally uninterested will not be helpful in maintaining an effective coaching conversation. Also, beware of what you are doing with your hands! The body language of the coachee can tell you much that is not being said. If they slump, pace about, avoid eye contact, wring their hands, run their hand through their hair, fiddle with items of clothing or pens and so on – all of this *may* be telling you something. Equally, it may not – but being aware of it is the first step, knowing if it means something is the second, and knowing how to use it appropriately in the coaching conversation is the third.

2.4   Number Four – **MOBILITY**

There is a scale of coaching approaches ranging from *I Tell You* – that is, the conversation has its centre in *my own* experience – to *I Listen with You* – that is, the conversation has its centre in *your* experience. A skilful, capable coach has mobility when they can seamlessly and unconsciously move between their own experience and that of the coachee's, in service of the coachee's goals.

Because some heavy-handed and manipulative coaching sounds like 'Tell' *(do this, don't do that)*, being centred in my own experience is often regarded as manipulative and being centred in the coachee's experience is often seen as 'client-centred'. This is not necessarily the case. Very occasionally, telling someone what to do, giving an instruction or passing on some feedback is the best way of helping the coachee to perform to their best without belittling or manipulating them in any way.

As a rule, coaching that is centred in the coachee's own experience is more effective, as it allows the individual to *discover* and *own* new learning, which is why open questions are so effective in performance coaching. However, interventions that are centred in my own experience as coach – such as robust challenge and feedback – can be extremely powerful and insightful for the coachee.

When choosing where to centre the conversation (over here, in my experience; or over there, in the coachee's experience), it is crucial that the coach stops and checks what their *intent* is for any given intervention: am I giving the coachee the very best opportunity, right now, to raise awareness, learn and own this situation so they take committed action? Or am I simply getting off on my own power, authority, cleverness or need to perform or add value as a coach? These are all interferences for the coach and reduce our capacity to act effectively for the coachee.

CASE STUDY

A highly effective coach I know was asked recently by a CEO to give him a personal one-to-one experience of non-directive coaching. The CEO was considering bringing coaching into the organisation but had not experienced it first-hand, although he had had some experience of being mentored by an external consultant.

The coach asked the CEO what he wanted coaching on (an issue around communication in his top team) and for the following half-hour the coach listened and gave sensible advice and suggestions. When she felt the conversation had run its course, the coach then asked the CEO how he felt about the effectiveness of the session. The CEO said although he now had five actions, he had slightly resented being told what to do, felt demoralised and did not really have a lot of faith that the actions would have much impact on his issue.

The coach acknowledged this and asked if the CEO would be prepared to have a second conversation for a further half-hour period. This time the coach listened in a different way – not to spot and offer help or solutions, but to create a listening environment where the CEO could start to understand his own thoughts about the issue.

The atmosphere was much lighter. There was more laughter and energy. At the end of the half-hour, the coach asked the CEO to sum up what he was going to do. He listed the same five actions as before and the coach pointed this out to him.

'Ah yes,' replied the CEO, 'but this time I have thought through all the connections and it makes *sense* to me now. I know exactly why I am taking action, what to do and when.' He immediately understood the power of non-directive coaching.

It usually does not help to tell other people what to do – they won't see it the way you do and your solution won't make *sense* to them. For the solution to make sense and to be owned by them, the individual needs to think it out for themselves.

The full range from listening to telling is appropriately available to the manager or coach, although once they become aware of the dynamics at play in the relationship, most realise that they have been centering the conversation in their own experience way too much. As human beings, we tend to listen for the space into which we can insert our advice. This says a lot about us, but disempowers the speaker from discovering their own thinking and taking responsibility for action. As Baz Lehrman says, 'advice is a form of nostalgia' – advice makes us feels good about ourselves, but it is usually an automatic response from our ego, rather than given out of our authentic choice in service of another.

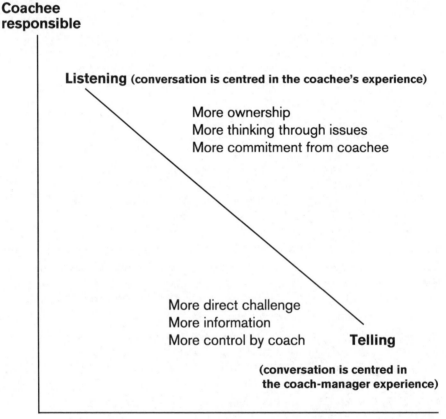

Coachee responsible

Listening (conversation is centred in the coachee's experience)

More ownership
More thinking through issues
More commitment from coachee

More direct challenge
More information
More control by coach   **Telling**

(conversation is centred in the coach-manager experience)

Coach responsible

Giving advice makes us feel good about ourselves. It makes us feel as though we are helping and it comes naturally – it is what we are all used to doing. But giving advice does not usually help as much as letting the other person take responsibility for finding the answer for themselves.

Choosing to centre the conversation in the coach or manager's own experience can be very effective for the coachee:

- in very urgent or stressful situations when immediate action must be taken;
- when the risks outweigh the benefits and you have concerns that the coachee might harm themselves or others if not given specific advice;
- when you are the only person who has certain knowledge or information that need to be transferred (e.g. legal, technical);
- when giving specific feedback, particularly around impact and feelings;
- when as leader you need to take a decision.

Effective coaches almost always begin by centering the conversation in the coachee's experience – just trying to understand their world and opening up the listening space – and finding that their own experience is usually of little help or value to the coachee (although of course, the *process* of coaching is of immense value). However, by momentarily centering the conversation in their own experience, a coach can let their own wisdom, intuition and hypothesis come into the dialogue and potentially add to the process. For example, they might direct the coachee's attention towards a particular thing using statements such as:

- I think it would be helpful if you focused on your relationship with X...
- I'd like you to put your attention on this particular area of your 360° feedback results...
- Can I suggest that you look at this particular area of your work...
- I notice you've mentioned X three times and each time, you've looked sad...
- My intuition is telling me that we should spend more time considering...

Here is an example of directing attention from the classic text *Zen and the Art of Motorcycle Maintenance* by Robert Pirsig*. While teaching rhetoric at an American college, the protagonist, Phaedrus, becomes fascinated (and subsequently obsessed) by the meaning of 'quality' in his work. At one stage, a female student is attempting to write a 500-word essay about the United States. The student, who has a reputation for diligence but also for spectacular lack of creativity, can think of nothing to say and is upset. Phaedrus suggests that she narrow it down to the local town. She returns, even more upset, still with nothing to say. Then he suggests that she narrow it down to just the main street of the local town – surely she can think of something to say about that? Still nothing. As Pirsig writes:

> He was furious. 'You're not looking!' he said ... 'For every fact there is an infinity of hypotheses. The more you look the more you see ... Narrow it down to the front of one building on the main street ... the Opera House. Start with the upper left hand brick.'

> She came in the next class with a puzzled look and handed in a five thousand word essay on the front of the Opera House on the main street. (p. 185)

[* Published by The Bodley Head. Reprinted by permission of The Random House Group Ltd.]

This focusing of attention improves the coachee's focus by getting them to put their attention on areas which you, as coach, have noticed recurring in their behaviour, but which the coachee cannot see for themselves.

Tests of intent

In his excellent book *Effective Coaching*, Myles Downey suggests four tests of intent which will help the coach to appreciate in the moment of speaking whether their intervention, be it directive or non-directive, is in service of the coachee. Does the intervention:

- raise the awareness of the coachee?
- generate responsibility in the coachee to take action?
- leave choice with the coachee to think through the issue and act for themselves?
- maintain the relationship of trust and respect between coachee and coach?

Questions the coach might ask of themselves include the following:

- Whose agenda of interest am I following here?
- Is my intent driven by my own interest to be right, look good or manipulate?
- Am I genuinely following the interests of the coachee by focusing their attention on something which, as coach, I know will serve them?
- Is the way I'm feeling about the coachee right now (e.g. anxious, irritated, bored, frustrated, impatient) influencing how directive I am being and, if so, how?

By distinguishing what they are listening for, the coach can sideline their personal interferences continually and so maintain their listening as a clearing for possibility, focused entirely on the coachee. Typical interferences for a coach might be:

- power or personal agenda;
- wanting to be right;
- fear of getting it wrong;
- trying to help;
- having answers;
- trying to be a coach;
- looking smart or clever;
- lack of courage or confidence;
- needing a result or getting attached to outcome.

I cannot get inside your head and you cannot get into mine. The best we can do is to understand each other's worldview and not to judge it in any way because it does not accord with our own. In order to understand another's worldview we must be genuinely interested in them and it – not to confirm our own view, but in order to *learn* – a good coach is someone who is *listening to learn.*

2.5   Number Five – **INTUITION**

Everyone has had a 'gut feeling' about something, or the sense that something is wrong (or right) without knowing why or having any obvious indicators. Some say that intuition is the sixth sense; I personally believe that intuition is simply when we tap into a higher level of awareness and for a moment, more data is available to us than is normally the case. Whatever it is, it clearly exists and the use of intuition or 'gut feeling' by the coach in coaching can be very valuable.

Using intuition in coaching is very much an art and acquired through practice, although it is probably true to say that some people are naturally more intuitive than others. In the Myers-Briggs Type Indicator, intuition is the 'N' in the Sensing–Intuition preference pair. It indicates a preference for seeing 'the big picture', focusing on the relationships and connections between people and things rather than the facts or events themselves, and that a person is tuned into emerging possibility (this is *not* to say that people with a Sensing preference for facts and details do not make for excellent coaches!)

My definition of intuition is wider, and would include the capacity to know or understand an event or relationship via a process which cannot be explained logically or rationally. It is a core coaching competence recognised by the International Coaching Federation. In its competence category 'Coaching Presence', a subcategory is: 'accesses own intuition and trusts one's inner knowing – goes with the gut'. The capacity to be comfortable with intuitive leaps as well as the capability to ground facts and data at the same time is a highly developed skill which has to be acquired over time, with practice.

> *People with high levels of personal mastery ... set out to integrate reason and intuition and cannot afford to choose between their head and heart, any more than they would choose to walk on one leg or see with one eye.*
> — Peter Senge, *Presence*, p. 144

Of course, intuition is related to sight, touch, taste, smell and hearing. These senses are physical and in psychological terms (psychosynthesis), the physical sensations are linked with intuition as well as four further 'functions' to make up the six functions:

- intuition;
- physical sensations (sight, touch, taste, smell and hearing);
- feelings;
- thoughts;
- desires and impulses; and
- imagination.

The more self-aware we are in these six functions, the more readily we will be able to access our intuitive side, as they are all related. In psychological terms, these six functions are different facets of the Self: 'I' am conscious of myself in the world and interact with it through these functions.

Intuition is the non-verbal communication we pick up, all the stuff that the left side of the brain ignores because it is too busy 'talking' to itself. In stillness and attentive listening, intuition and logic are fused – we consciously notice what previously we would have missed. Higher levels of personal awareness allow our intuition to emerge. Intuition is a 'muscle' which can be exercised and developed. For example, the American psychologist Marc Salem demonstrates an uncanny ability to 'read people's minds'. He explains:

> *I am constantly picking up cues that provide me with information. People let half the world go by without even paying attention to it ... if we make ourselves more aware, we have better lives. We don't have to feel like we're searching, when the facts and the answers are right there in front of us.*
> — Holland, 'It's Funny You Think That', *The London Newspaper*,
> 19 July 2007, p. 13

I really agree with this statement. I think it is certainly the case that increased awareness of ourselves and the world around us through our six functions hugely increases our understanding of what we are individually and how we are in our relationships with others. This awareness can reshape our choices, responses and results. Whether you look at this from the perspective of being a coach, work colleague, friend, parent or teacher, it has to be worthwhile paying attention to *paying attention*. As Professor Richard Wiseman states:

> *The ability to accurately judge the emotions of others is an essential psychological skill in almost every area of life.*

2.6   Number Six – **NORMS**

By 'norms', I mean boundaries. To be effective, coaching conversations must remain within certain limits, which are defined by the following:
- the contract;
- the capability of the coach (skills, training, areas of competence);
- the relationship between coach and coachee; and
- the coachee's own boundaries.

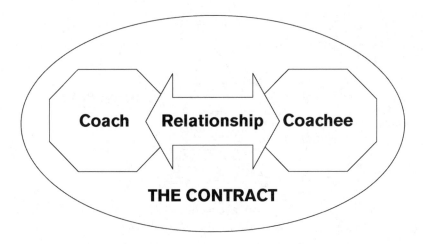

The contract

Coaching does not take place in a vacuum. There is a background organisational context which will include:

- the cultural norms of the organisation (values, leadership style, management style, communication expectations, and so on);
- organisational understanding and expectations of coaching – what it is and is not, who the key stakeholders are, and how it fits into day-to-day management;
- expectations of improved results and how to evaluate the process.

Capability of the coach

Coaching is not counselling. Simplistically, counselling is about making the past more bearable and understandable for the client so they can move forward and be more capable in the present. Coaching is about understanding the present more fully and with greater insight so that the coachee can move forward and be more capable in the future. Of course, the present is always informed by the past and the skill of the coach is to raise awareness around only those issues which directly impinge on – or interfere with – the individual's performance now.

A coach will find ways round issues, while a counsellor or therapist will be interested in the issue itself. This is fine if that is the contract – but in coaching, it is not.

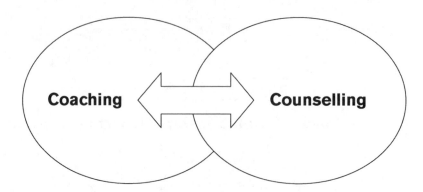

It is very easy to get sucked into a coachee's story and if the relationship is strong, the individual may feel able to share some deep and long-held personal issues which would not be appropriate in the coaching context and which the coach, unless professionally trained, could not contain safely and appropriately.

Coaching must be a safe space and the boundaries of this space must be a number one priority. With so many managers now coaching in organisations, the supervision of managers or coaches is now a big organisational issue (see p. 27 on the coaching supervision of coaches and managers). When a coach comes up against this issue for themselves, they are usually in conversation alone with the coachee. Given that the coach has sensibly spent time on their personal boundary awareness, they should be confident in knowing when their instincts or observations tell them to call a halt to the coaching. Permission to do this will have been established already in the contract.

'Avoiding the Titanic Syndrome': how to recognise a coaching boundary and what to do then

When confronted by an apparent counselling or therapy issue in coaching, it is important to acknowledge rather than ignore it. However, the issue should not be picked apart as it might in a therapy or counselling session, as coaching is neither of these things and the line must not be crossed.

Imagine you and the coachee are on a ship, sailing across the 'Sea of Their Awareness', when you come across an iceberg in the conversation – let's call it the 'Iceberg of Low Self-esteem'. This could be a small iceberg – many people have some self-esteem issues which, with practice and coaching, they work through very successfully – but a minority of people have very difficult self-esteem issues which may refer to, for example, occurrences in their childhood or their personal experience of being parented. This may well occur as a large iceberg and be inappropriate for tackling in a coaching session, whether the coach has skill or qualifications in therapy or not, as their contract is for coaching.

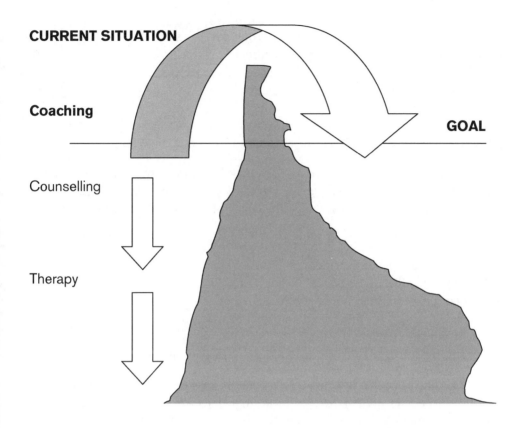

CURRENT SITUATION

Coaching

GOAL

Counselling

Therapy

The skilful coach will spend sufficient time understanding the iceberg – taking depth soundings, so to speak, by listening and asking questions – to move the conversation on to the appropriate next stage. The point is to move quickly and effectively *around* the iceberg, not to get off the ship and spend time analysing the thing.

Coaching is goal-oriented – there is a destination to get to in the most effective way, which will be timeframed, and stopping halfway to analyse icebergs is not within the remit. That said, if the issue is a real block to progress, something must be done to help the coachee begin to deal with it and to move forward. Part of the coaching conversation then will be around how best the coachee can take action for themselves to move forward – who could they speak to, what help do they need and how could they get it. The coach may well offer some advice as well at this point – the names or contacts of appropriate helping organisations, for example, offers of support or referral, and so on.

Recognising the signs
Recognition falls into two main areas: internal and external signals. There will be *internal* signals for the coach which they feel or intuit about the coachee. Typically these will express themselves in the coach as:

- concern for physical safety (their own or the coachee's);
- concern for the mental health of the coachee;
- strong emotions in the coach such as fear, sadness, anger;
- anxiety or self-doubt;
- feelings of sympathy;
- the need to rescue the coachee;
- feelings of panic or inability.

Internal signals can be deceptive as they may be more about the needs of the coach than the coachee. However, recognition may be clearer when or if combined with *external* signals which the coach observes in the coachee, such as:

- excessively passive or aggressive body language;
- rapid breathing, raised voice;
- shouting or excessive swearing;
- illogical or incoherent responses to questions;
- unusual (i.e. more than normal) expressions of emotion;
- crying, if this appears more than a normal expression;
- little or no eye contact;
- flushing, perspiring or other possible signs of discomfort.

Of course, most healthy and mentally fit people get angry or cry occasionally (it does not mean they are psychotic!). In itself, a few tears or a raised voice do not constitute a boundary issue for the coach unless it indicates a pattern that concerns the coach. However, the competent coach must be able to ensure the safety and well-being of the coachee, and needs to maintain vigilance in this area in order to maintain safety in the coaching relationship.

	INNER	OUTER
COACH	What do I notice about my own feelings, thoughts and imaginings?	What do I *see* about myself physically or *hear* myself saying or style of language – specific words
COACHEE	What can I intuit about the coachee's frame of mind? Test – ask questions to check their inner dialogue	What do I *see* about the coachee physically in terms of body language or *hear* – such as words they use, silence and so on

The coach has to access their own inner dialogue and may observe their own outer behaviours as well as the outer behaviours of the coachee. What is less accessible to the coach is the inner dialogue of the coachee – what are *they* thinking, feeling or imagining? This is when the coach may intuit something going on; however, there is only one way to be sure of what is going on in someone's mind: that is, to ask them.

If the coach has a real cause to be concerned for the welfare of their coachee during a coaching session, they should consider their options to:

- stop the coaching conversation appropriately;
- say what they feel and notice about the coachee that gives them cause for concern;
- explain that this is beyond the agreed boundaries (remind them of the contract if necessary) and that the conversation needs to move elsewhere more helpful for the coachee;
- ask the coachee what they would like to do now in terms of where they would like to move the conversation;
- provide some appropriate input, such as recommending helping organisations, a counsellor or therapist, or helping to find out about occupational health schemes, and so on;
- liaise with the subsequent counsellor or therapist and coachee regarding the possibility of continuing coaching at an appropriate time.

Relationship between coach and coachee

The coaching relationship is one where there exists a high level of rapport. In such relationships, it is well understood that a number of different dynamics can occur, for example:

- power can shift from the coachee to the coach and for the relationship to edge towards that of a parent and child;
- the relationship becomes over-friendly and loses its value-added edge of performance challenge;
- the relationship becomes very friendly and veers towards one of a physical or even sexual nature.

The coach must be on their guard at all times against behaviour occurring in the relationship which does not meet the highest ethical and professional standards. The contract will help to clarify some of these boundaries.

The coachee's own boundaries

The coachee will always have their own personal boundaries which, in most cases, will prevent healthy coping adults from overstepping either their own or other agreed boundaries. Behaviour that is out of the norm and which implies that the coachee is indeed overstepping their personal boundaries would give the coach a real cause for concern, and would be a signal to stop the conversation (as described previously).

CASE STUDY

Several years ago I was asked by the human resources (HR) manager of an investment bank to coach an executive in the London office. The individual, I was told, was struggling to meet targets and 'needed some remedial coaching' after 18 months in the job. Alarm bells began to ring in my mind.

I met with the manager and subsequently with the individual to get as full a picture as I could of the context. It was certainly apparent that the individual's performance had slipped over the last 12 months. It also became apparent to me that little had been said or done by the individual's manager, or the manager's manager (whom we shall call 'M2'), to point this out and take remedial action. The manager, so I discovered, had a reputation for favouritism and poor management. The HR department seemed to be taking a passive approach.

I agreed to have two further diagnostic meetings, one with the individual and one with their line manager. My request to speak to M2 was declined on the grounds that she was travelling. It emerged from these meetings that appraisals had not been done, one-to-one meetings cancelled and communication was at a minimum. The manager seemed to think that the individual was verging on incompetent and recruited in error – much my own feelings about the manager at the time. The individual was stressed and felt very undervalued and undermined by certain behaviours exhibited by the manager.

I returned to the HR manager and told him that I declined to coach the individual at this time, that they needed support from HR, and possibly occupational health. I said the issue was a management one and would only be resolved when the manager adopted a different approach to managing. My offer of services in this regard was politely declined.

Had I accepted the original brief, I would have found myself almost certainly embroiled in the power politics of the manager and tacitly engaged in a covert exit strategy for the individual – a position incompatible with the integrity and transparency of good coaching.

2.7 Number Seven – ACTION-ORIENTATION

Efforts and courage are not without purpose and direction.

— John F. Kennedy

If coaching is about anything, it is about getting in action. This does not necessarily mean gung-ho action (although it could, of course, and often does), but it does mean taking responsibility for one's feelings and thoughts, putting them into perspective, evaluating one's attitude and behaviours in the light of feedback and planning and taking action to become more effective at whatever game we are playing (whether football, work, parenting or life).

Response starts at the deeper level of feelings and could mean:

- a new way of looking at a problem or relationship from now on;
- an authentic commitment to avoid a certain behaviour or action in the future;
- seeing the world in a different frame.

AN EXAMPLE OF REFRAMING

My family was recently offered the chance of going on a week's skiing holiday with a wealthy relative; he generously said that he would pay for all the hotel bills, food and accommodation and airport and hotel transfers. I leapt at the chance of what I perceived at the time as a free holiday for the four of us.

What I had not considered was the cost of airport parking, ski equipment hire, ski passes and tuition (which we desperately needed), plus the cost of incidental food and drinks during the day. At this particular resort, all this added up to a substantial amount of money. By the end of day two I found myself slightly resenting my generous host – this 'free' holiday was costing me a fortune!

Then it occurred to me that he never said it was free – just generously subsidised. When I began to reframe the holiday in this light, it became obvious to me that actually it was a tremendous 'bargain' as a holiday, which otherwise we could never have afforded as a family. I went from grumpy to grateful in one second, and from then on thoroughly enjoyed the holiday and the generosity of our host – my behaviours and actions became congruent with the new frame I had created.

We often think that we are in action when we are not. What does this mean? Take, for example, people watching a football match or a game of tennis. They will have comments, views, opinions and no doubt a lot to say about the skill (or lack of it) of the players on pitch or court. This is perfectly natural, as they themselves are playing a game – that of spectator. However, the role of spectator is a passive one and without responsibility for any of the action on the pitch or court. In effect, the role of spectator is a permission to moan, opinionate or cheer, but always secondhand – it is someone or something else we are talking about and we are, in effect, disengaged from the action.

The role of the coach is to engage the coachee in action on the pitch or court and bring them out of the stands. For the duration of play, no more opinions, moans or complaints about the rules, just get into play – which is reminiscent of Nike's motto, 'Just Do It'. When we feel sorry for ourselves or we feel let down, angry, disappointed, hurt, unappreciated, gloomy or depressed – these are actually self-inflicted wounds, which the coach will help the player to explore and overcome as quickly as possible, bearing in mind appropriate boundaries (see 'Norms'), and to get back into action again.

Coaching that does not result in some kind of action is simply a pleasant chat. There is nothing wrong with that, but don't mistake it for coaching. By definition, nothing happens without action. However, there is a vital ingredient to action that makes it more or less effective – and that ingredient is commitment.

Commitment

We have forty million reasons for failure but not a single excuse.

— Rudyard Kipling

As someone once said, there is always another dirty cup in the sink. It is easy to put things off, to find an excuse or create a reason why something did not happen ('there was another cup to wash').

If something really has your commitment, then you will do it, come hell or high water. You may not get the result you expected – you may get more, not as much as you were hoping for, or even something completely different – but you will get much more than you would have otherwise.

An effective coach will hold their coachees to their commitments and help them to understand what is holding them back from stepping further onto the court. The coach is there to help the player play their best game, and as coach they are committed to the player's commitment. By holding themselves 'committed to the commitment' rather than specifically to the player, the coach can remain impartial and avoid the pitfall of sympathy rather than empathy.

Stretch goals

Commitments vary from the easy ('I will meet you at the cinema at 7pm without fail') to the difficult ('I will quadruple turnover for this division in one year'). This latter may be fairly simple if there are plenty of resources, or it may be an outrageous statement which has no ground in historic evidence. High-stretch coaches favour the latter, where commitments are made from the ground of what is wanted or needed, not from the ground of what is available and likely. Standing in the future, coach and coachee agree the ideal result and work back from there, filling in the gaps by doing what is needed to achieve the result 'from the future'.

The stretch target might be extremely high, but that in itself is irrelevant. The purpose of a high-stretch goal is to create the conditions for transformational change, which of course has to occur in the individual before it is seen in the world as action and results. High-stretch goals are a commitment, not a promise, and they demand the performer not only to do different things and to think in new ways, but to challenge their own perceptions of self on a rollercoaster journey of self-discovery, captured in Anatole Broyard's quote:

The wonder, the terror, the exaltation of being on the edge of being.

High-stretch goals or commitments must catch the breath with their audacity and the coachee must always feel free to accept or decline. Acceptance does not mean taking on a burden; rather it should be seen as a great opportunity for discovery and development, facilitated by the coach, that always results in learning and higher achievement and usually produces truly outstanding, and occasionally unexpected, results. Great performers at their peak of excellence describe the sensation of 'being in flow' where their actions are perfectly tuned to the task, and all sense of self-doubt and self-consciousness disappear. In this mental state, it is the exhilaration of playing the 'game' that matters – they are focused, relaxed, completely engaged and achieving their full potential as a human being. The wonderful thing is that this mental state, perfect for peak performance, is available to everyone: it just needs something at stake, a commitment to succeed, perseverance – and a coach!

Security is mostly superstition. It does not exist in nature nor do the children of men as a whole experience it. Avoiding danger is no safer in the long run than outright exposure. Life is either a daring adventure or nothing.

— Helen Keller

2.8   Number Eight – **SUPPORT**

To support another person means:

- understanding clearly what the other person is attempting to succeed in (their goal) and what the perceived obstacles may be to achieving it;
- appreciating what success means to them (their motivation);
- being personally committed to their success;
- believing they can succeed, even when they themselves may not.

These are the *compass points of support* and you need to be attentive to all four points in order to genuinely show you are supporting another person. If you pretend to understand their objective or their motivation but really don't, your lack of clarity will show up as lack of interest. If you are not too bothered about their succeeding, or don't believe they can, your attitude will come across and demotivate them.

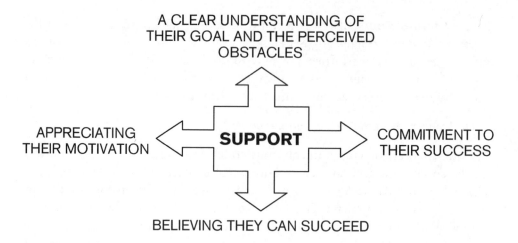

A CLEAR UNDERSTANDING OF
THEIR GOAL AND THE PERCEIVED
OBSTACLES

APPRECIATING
THEIR MOTIVATION

SUPPORT

COMMITMENT TO
THEIR SUCCESS

BELIEVING THEY CAN SUCCEED

Listening for understanding and motivation

When we listen to other people, we are generally listening for confirmation of our own ideas or alignment to our own worldview. We all have our own way of seeing the world and it can be upsetting, irritating or confusing when we hear others challenging or disagreeing with what we hold as true and 'right'.

> *Usually, when you listen to some statement, you hear it as a kind of echo of yourself. You are actually listening to your own opinion. If it agrees with your opinion, you may accept it, but if it does not, you will reject it, or not ever really hear it.* — Shunryu Suzuki Roshi, Japanese sage

Our listening becomes a filter to our conscious minds as we grow up and it is difficult for us to really listen without filtering everything we hear through our preconceptions, personal values, prejudices and preferences. Yet if we can put these to one side as we listen to another, we can hear far more than before and create a space for mutual understanding and appreciation. In this space we can ask questions for clarification that come from a genuine desire to understand rather than to control or impose.

It becomes much easier to appreciate what is motivating them and they will feel that they are being appreciated for who they are, rather than just for what they are saying.

CASE STUDY

I once ran a three-day workshop for senior managers in a large accountancy firm. This group specialised in auditing accounts. I began a group exercise which started with telling the group a true experience I had had as a coach.

At intervals I knocked a spoon against a glass, their signal to note down individually their level of attention to me on a scale of 1 to 10, and a one-word memo of where their attention had wandered to, if it wasn't a 10. After six or seven minutes I stopped the exercise and asked the group for a sense of the scores.

Most started high – 7 or 8 – then there was a startling drop to almost zero across the group. The scores remained bumping across the bottom, until I had mentioned what sounded to them like statistical data, at which point the group's attention soared as one. Something they could audit!

As soon as the group realised that the figures I was mentioning could not be audited, their listening – again uncannily as one – sank like a stone to level 1 or 2. Typical descriptors of where their attention had gone included:

- This is boring...
- What's his point?
- He's rambling...
- Where's this going?
- Where did he get that tie?
- When's lunch?!

It eventually sank in that all this was simply a listening they had for *themselves* – driven by their own need to be entertained, interested and engaged, as though that were the responsibility of the speaker.

Of course, to be an engaging speaker I need to interest and enrol others, but the specific role of the *listener* is to be responsible for their listening – to *be* interested and attentive to another, regardless of the content.

It was an insightful moment for many of the group, who realised how little they truly listened to their clients and staff.

Believing they can succeed and commitment to their success

A belief is something you hold to be true, no matter what the evidence is to the contrary. Sometimes there is a fair bit of evidence to suggest that the person in front of you is a complete 'dork' (and they may be thinking the same about you), and this then becomes yet another filter in your listening (and theirs).

What is needed here is the faith to believe that this person:

- is capable of achieving whatever they put their mind and effort to;
- has the resources within themselves to succeed;
- is not achieving anything even remotely near their true potential;
- is free to choose to what they want to commit their energy and resources.

Having these beliefs isn't a skill, but a *capacity* – the capacity to hold open a possibility for another person, even when they cannot hold it themselves. If you can hold these beliefs in an honest and authentic way and behave accordingly, you will be offering them the very best support. Someone who is really effective at supporting other people on all the four compass points of support mentioned above will demonstrate the following kinds of behaviours:

- asking clear, concise questions to deepen mutual understanding;
- listening with attention and accuracy and demonstrating this in their attentive body language, their ability to summarise accurately and reflect appropriately, and showing continued interest in the desired outcomes for the person;
- not backing away from giving tough feedback if it will help the person to reach their goal;
- demonstrating their appreciation of the difficulties and challenges that the person is facing, through expressing their empathy;
- holding the line and not backing away from or diluting the goal if it begins to seem too daunting for the person – this is when they need the coach most.

3 What's your coaching style?

3.1 THE STAMINAS QUESTIONNAIRE

The following questionnaire will help you to discover which one of four main coaching styles you have. You may find that you have a preference for one style with some additional leanings towards another. The intention is to help you raise your awareness around your coaching preferences, develop your strengths and choose which areas you feel could be valuable for you to develop as a coach. The questionnaire is *not* a scientific instrument and is not intended as anything more than an indicator for your own interest and potential development as a coach.

The eight STAMINAS are:
- *Structuring* – the skills of creating the structure and rigour that effective coaching conversations need;
- *Toughness* – the capacity to challenge and give direct feedback;
- *Affinity* – the capacity to create and sustain strong empathetic relationships that engender trust, responsibility and respect;
- *Mobility* – the capacity of self-awareness to appreciate when and how to use a range of approaches, from the non-directive to the directive, in service of the client;
- *Intuition* – using feelings and instincts as well as other senses to understand the coachee and the dynamics of the relationship, in order to raise awareness;
- *Norms* – appreciation and application of boundaries and the ethical principles of effective coaching;
- *Action-orientation* – seeking beneficial outcomes with the coachee that create commitment to action and a significant improvement in results, however measured; and
- *Support* – the capacity to create an environment of mutual understanding and to hold an authentic commitment to another's success.

There are 64 statements (eight statements for each of the eight STAMINAS). Respond to each statement by agreeing or disagreeing with the statement. If you agree with the statement more than you disagree with it, tick it. If you disagree with the statement more than you agree with it, put a cross by it. You should tick or cross every statement. If you are not sure, go on to the next statement, but be sure to return to unfinished responses and either tick or cross them.

There are no right or wrong responses to the statements – the questionnaire simply indicates what your preferential coaching style might be. Although there is no time limit, don't take too long or think too hard before responding to each statement, your initial response will be fine. Remember, this is for you and is about your style, so be as honest and real as you can.

The questionnaire

1) At work most of my conversations have specific, usually measurable, outcomes.
2) I am good at facts and data and explore these when coaching others.
3) I am quite competitive and want the coachee to get on.
4) I often get a gut feeling about an issue or a person.
5) I am usually very clear on measures and success factors in my coaching.
6) I present facts as I see them, even if the coachee finds it uncomfortable.
7) I find it difficult to give people tough feedback.
8) I tend to focus on the people issues in coaching.
9) I may avoid pushing or challenging if I think it will cause an upset.
10) I tend to ask more questions than other people when in conversation.
11) Once I understand a coachee's limitations, I won't push them further.
12) I like to vary my coaching – venue, style, timings and so on.
13) I can often find myself pessimistic or problem-focused when coaching.
14) I don't mind being unpopular if it gets results.
15) I am good at seeing the bigger picture when coaching.
16) I generally get a sense of shape to a conversation and can get back on track if distracted.
17) I am very effective at holding people to their commitments.
18) I often see different ways of helping or working with clients.
19) I find it uncomfortable to hold people to account.
20) I am very particular to start and finish conversations on time.
21) When coaching, I can find myself talking about ideas or new possibilities.
22) I generally have highly structured coaching conversations.
23) I know when to tell and when to listen, and I'm accomplished at switching.
24) I have no problem in giving tough feedback.
25) I have a tendency for future focus in my coaching.
26) I often find my hunches are correct when speaking with people.
27) I am sympathetic when people complain about their difficulties.
28) I like using different tools and models when coaching.
29) I tend to feel upset when I know that my coaching is very challenging.
30) I am inclined to help the coachee see a need for change.
31) When coaching, I often notice physical sensations that have no apparent cause.

32) I tend to encourage coachees to weigh up facts and information and to check them before acting. ✗

33) I like to have access to documents and reports which might add data to my coaching, and feel under-informed if I can't get it. ✗

34) I am quite assertive and pushy in coaching, particularly with people who can't make up their minds what to do. ✗

35) My coaching diary schedule tends to be very organised and planned well in advance – deviations annoy me. ✗

36) I will try to get to the nub of the issue as quickly as possible. ✓

37) I like to follow my instinct rather than rely too heavily on data. ✓

38) I feel it is important that my coachees like me. ✗

39) I am always clear about the purpose of a coaching conversation and the outcomes that are expected. ✓

40) I tend to be focused on the present or short term when coaching. ✓

41) I very rarely feel sympathetic towards a coachee. ✗

42) I enjoy conversations that have a specific outcome and action. ✓

43) I am good at seeing short-term problems when coaching. ✓

44) I can get bored quite easily when coaching other people. ✓

45) My style is relaxed towards non-delivery if there is a good reason for it. ✓

46) I have a reputation for getting on with people. ✓

47) I am efficient and enjoy producing client meeting reports and documentation. ✗

48) The coachee's personal fears do not overly concern me as coach. ✗

49) I feel very aware of my own gut feelings when I am coaching people and often act on these feelings. ✗

50) I tend to be interested in the coachee's past history and their relationships. ✗

51) I am able to put my opinions of people and their reputation to one side. ✓

52) I am sensitive to the impact of the coachee's action on their relationships. ✓

53) I am less interested in feelings and more interested in hard facts and data. ✗

54) I get irritated by people who have excuses why they didn't do something. ✗

55) People tell me that I am an intuitive person. ✓

56) I think about my coachee's immediate situation with logical precision, often producing working hypotheses. ✗

57) I am often aware of another's pain or sorrow and want to help them if I can. ✓

58) I am usually quite challenging and forthright when I coach. ✓

59) I think I am more effective as a coach if people like me and I like them. ✓

60) I am comfortable giving my own opinion when asked for it by the coachee. ✓

61) I use a wide range of tools, techniques and different approaches when coaching. ✓

62) I like coaching people who get on with things and are task-oriented. ✗

63) I am often more gratified to have positive feedback about my relationship with the coachee than about specific results. ✗

64) My own preference is for doing rather than thinking. ✗

Scoring the questionnaire

Add up your total score, scoring one point for every tick and no points for any cross.

STAMINAS	Statement number	Total
Structure	1, 5, 10, 16, 20, 22, 39, 42	6
Toughness	6, 14, 17, 24, 41, 48, 54, 58	3
Affinity	7, 8, 9, 11, 19, 27, 29, 38	4
Mobility	12, 13, 18, 21, 23, 28, 30, 61	5
Intuition	4, 15, 25, 26, 31, 37, 49, 55	4
Norms	2, 32, 33, 35, 47, 53, 56, 60	1
Action-orientation	3, 34, 36, 40, 43, 44, 62, 64	5
Support	45, 46, 50, 51, 52, 57, 59, 63	6

Now pair up and add your scores in the following way:

Intuition and Mobility 9	Toughness and Action-orientation 8	Support and Affinity 10	Norms and Structuring 7
Total: 9	Total: 8	Total: 10	Total: 7
CREATIVE orientation	OFFENSIVE orientation	RELATIONAL orientation	EMPIRICAL orientation

Scores more than 11 indicate a *strong preference* for a style.

Scores between 7 and 10 indicate a *moderate preference* for a style.

Scores between 3 and 6 indicate a *low preference* for a style.

Scores between 0 and 2 indicate a *very low preference* for a style.

Plotting your scores

Use the chart below to plot your score, where 0 is at the centre and 16 is at the tip of the diagonal arrows.

3.2 THE FOUR MAIN CORE COACHING STYLES

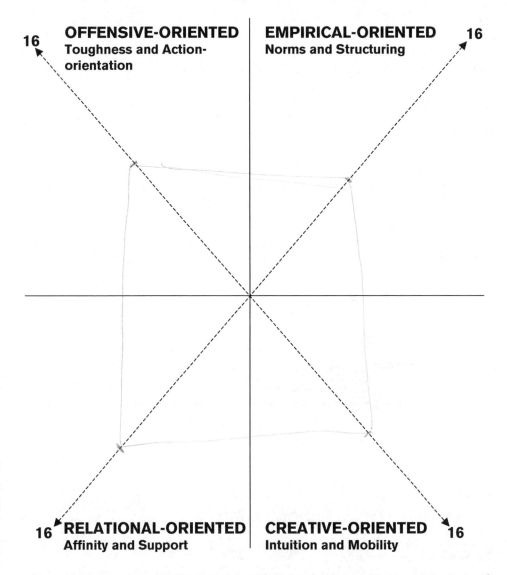

OFFENSIVE-ORIENTED
Toughness and Action-orientation

EMPIRICAL-ORIENTED
Norms and Structuring

16

16

RELATIONAL-ORIENTED
Affinity and Support

CREATIVE-ORIENTED
Intuition and Mobility

16

16

(Core model adapted from Thinking Styles, *Leadership 101* by Margaret Lloyd and Brian Rothwell)

The most effective coaches will have the ability to move with agility across all four stylistic types of coach in order to provide the most appropriate intervention for the coachee – that is, the approach that will help the coachee to become more aware, self-enabled and in action towards their goals. Knowing our personal style preference gives us the opportunity to work on our less preferred styles to become more rounded – and more effective – in our coaching approach.

The Creative-oriented coach

Your style

As a creative-oriented coach, you use your intuition and innate creativity with more ease and flexibility than other coaches. You will find particular resonance with the sections in this book on Mobility and Intuition. You may well use a number of imaginative coaching approaches and vary your coaching with drawing, role-play, modelling, sculpting and so on.

You will tend to view the coaching you do as facilitating the coachee's journey in itself, looking towards a bigger picture, and as a result you might be less focused on specific results. You have a strong future focus and the 'here and now' can feel constraining when coaching – on occasions this can lead to a problem rather than a solution focus. You will have the capability to help the coachee find numerous options to move forward, but may be less helpful in confirming a specific action plan and less effective than you could be in gaining commitment. Your focus will tend to be more on strategy and less on task and action.

Least preferred style: empirical

As a creative-oriented coach, you may find the rigour and process favoured by a coachee with an empirical style both limiting and calculating. You will be interested in creative coaching techniques that may feel flaky and lacking in rigour to your empirical coachee. On the other hand, effective coaching needs rigour and structure. You should become aware of any tendency mentioned above which might impact your effectiveness as a coach and work on these to develop a more rounded approach to your coaching. You could find working with coachees who have an empirical style themselves mildly irritating. You might not look forward to the sessions and this will show up in your coaching.

DEVELOPING YOUR CAPACITY:

- focus more on facts
- relate more to the coachee's past experience
- structure coaching sessions rigorously
- apply more problem-solving approaches when coaching
- apply your own thinking and occasionally offer hypotheses
- try relating more to the coachee
- be very clear on contracting issues and boundaries.

The Offensive-oriented coach

Your style

As an offensive-oriented coach, you will be very action-oriented (hence the use of the descriptor 'offensive', as in the dictionary definition 'for the purposes of attack, rather than defence'). You are not offensive; rather, you will be focused on the here and now and keen for the coachee to tackle problems promptly as they emerge. You can give tough feedback when appropriate and you can be quite willful as a coach, sometimes to the point of subduing a coachee, who on occasions may feel rather confronted by your approach.

You are very good at challenging and holding coachees to their commitments, but may be less effective at building deeper relationships with coachees or really appreciating their worldview. You are very results-focused and will appropriately challenge coachees, although you may appear directive at times. Your own need for action might cloud your judgement when the coachee could benefit from a more empathetic approach at the time.

Least preferred style: creative

As your preference is for action, you could find the wide lateral thinking of the creative style slow and passive and less focused on results. On the other hand, you may not be using your creative strengths fully, or drawing out those of your clients. You may find that when you are coaching creative people, you become impatient, even exasperated, at their lack of action or task focus. Guard against falling into this mindset by relaxing more and even trying out some more creative approaches in your coaching.

DEVELOPING YOUR CAPACITY:

- focus more on listening and appreciating the coachee's worldview
- focus more on longer-term futures and the big picture rather than the task
- try being less directive
- add some additional creative technique to your coaching
- take more time when coaching, slow down and take time to really understand what is going on for the coachee.

The Relational-oriented coach

Your style

As a relational-oriented coach, you will have highly-developed people skills and a high emotional intelligence quotient. You are very good at empathising with and understanding people and your coachees will feel comfortable and appreciated. Your conversations are often very deep, very honest and contain unusually high personal disclosure.

You will have an intuitive grasp of how an issue affects the various players in the organisation, not just the coachee, and this adds perspective and insight to your coaching. However, you may find it harder to give tough feedback, even when it is needed, and the level of challenge in your coaching may suffer as a result, which ultimately will not serve your client. Your need to be liked may prevent you from asserting your will when it is appropriate, and there lies the danger of tending towards cosy chats rather than performance conversations. You may find senior managers or individuals who are more assertive than you quite challenging to coach.

Least preferred style: offensive

Relational-oriented coaches can find the task and action-orientation of the offensive coach rather challenging, even unkind, and lacking in understanding of their situation. You might shy away from conflict and may occasionally fall into sympathy (rather than empathy), which would disempower both you and your client. When coaching action-oriented people, you might find it harder to relate to them and could find yourself trying to contain the conversation by over-structuring it, which in turn might frustrate your client who wants to be in action, not just dialogue.

DEVELOPING YOUR CAPACITY:

- you are good at matching, so try mismatching for a change. Be more assertive when you would normally be more quiet, assert more personal authority
- get more facts and data, such as 360° feedback, and use the data to give objective feedback
- be very clear on goals and coaching commitments and more rigorous in checking back on actions when you next meet the coachee
- raise the bar on challenge by encouraging the coachee to take bolder options and actions, which in turn will challenge you to be more challenging as coach
- introduce more energy in your coaching by varying the venue, using new techniques and creating more rigour in conversational structure.

The Empirical-oriented coach

Your style

As an empirical-oriented coach, you will be very competent at creating and maintaining appropriate contracts and boundaries for coaching, which includes all the paperwork and processes which many coaches often hate. You have a knack with facts and data and are very good at helping the coachee to see the factual information which they may have missed. You show considerable skill in structuring your coaching, both conversationally and in terms of clear outcomes and outputs, and can add valuable insight for the coachee from your own experience.

You might occasionally come across as clinical or unemotional and your interest in data, facts and logic might prevent you from creating the depth of coaching relationship which otherwise might have been possible. Your incisive thinking might prevent you from giving all your attention to the coachee, as you could be busy computing data in order to rebut, challenge or add to what the coachee has already said. You may find it more challenging to create conversations which have a future focus, particularly if there are potential risks that cannot be accurately assessed, or which fall outside of your own experience.

Least preferred style: relational

Your style of coaching is oriented towards boundaries and structure, both of which are absolutely necessary in coaching. You might find people with a more relational style intrusive, or that they tend to ask questions about feelings and emotions which might occur to you as uncomfortable or irrelevant, as you are interested more in facts than feelings. On the other hand, when coaching relational-oriented people, your tendency would be to try to 'oil the wheels' of the session by adding structure or creative techniques, rather than making the effort to appreciate their underlying emotions or feelings. This could confuse the client and make them feel that you are not really understanding or appreciating them. This might have the effect of putting up barriers in the conversation, rather than taking them down.

DEVELOPING YOUR CAPACITY:

- listen more to appreciate the personal concerns and anxieties of the coachee and demonstrate that you understand through summarising
- ask more 'feeling' questions and don't dismiss their answers – trust that there are 'golden nuggets' in what the coachee says, if only you could hear it
- try developing your intuitive side, go with gut instinct and be a bit more 'zany' in your coaching; go for an ice-cream break, for example
- try some new approaches, break the mould a little and introduce some humour and fun (appropriately).

3.3 HUMOUR IN COACHING

As a professional coach, I enjoy the experience of being coached and seek out such opportunities when I can. It is useful for my own performance and also hugely valuable for my own learning as a coach – there is no better place to learn about the effectiveness of certain coaching techniques and approaches than by sitting in the coachee's chair. Also, I get free coaching from some of the best coaches around which is, from my point of view, a rather neat bit of added value.

Recently I had such an opportunity as part of a learning set to which I belong. My coach for the session was an experienced, professional coach, someone I have worked with in the past occasionally and whose coaching skills are evident. The session took about 30 minutes and at the end of it I had to give the coach some feedback. I wondered what to say. On the one hand, my coach had demonstrated clear skill in structuring the conversation and was both empathic and rigorous. I had achieved my session goal and was committed to the few actions emerging – all good stuff. Unfortunately, the whole thing had been about as fun as watching paint dry.

This got me thinking (a rare event, for which I am grateful to the coach). I recalled many coaching demonstrations I either had done myself or witnessed and reflected on the numerous conversations with other professional coaches about our mutual coaching practice and the practices of the coaches I supervise. There was, and is, a trend: of being a *serious* coach – highly professional in approach (good), well-trained and at least literate in basic psychotherapy (good), and committed to adding value to the client (good). I know these people – I am one of them – and when they are not coaching, they can have me bent double with laughter (I can even bend myself double with laughter). However, often when we coach, it is as if a humour bypass kicks in, the fun and irreverence just drain away.

Of course, I am talking about the *appropriate and timely* use of humour. For example, the senior partner of an international law firm will not be too pleased if I turn up to coach wearing green baggy trousers and sporting a large plastic purple nose; cracking jokes or making light remarks will not match the senior executive stretched beyond breaking point due to work pressures. Witty coach-centred repartee should be left firmly outside the client's offices.

However, humour is one of the most powerful coaching levers. Edward de Bono says that 'humour is by far the most significant activity of the human brain'. In a recent *Guardian* article by Angela Balakrishnan he shows how a joke can display a switch in perception and how this is important in changing the way that we think. He goes on to say that 90% of error in thinking is due to error in perception. This has real significance in coaching, as there is a direct link between perception and performance. As individuals, it is the way we see the world, the way in which reality occurs to us in the moment, that shapes our immediate choices and actions. Humour can provide a shortcut to attitudinal or emotional shift for the coachee, and in that moment create more awareness, energy and scope for action.

De Bono's thinking on this issue is supported by Pattern Recognition Theory. An article in Metro (13 June 2008, Science and Discovery in Brief, MiniCosm, p. 14) states: 'Humour is a cognitive tool that plays a vital role in our mental development'. And that according to Pattern Recognition Theory, 'laughter occurs when the brain recognises a pattern that surprises it'. It quotes theorist Alastair Clarke saying that 'recognising such patterns help us develop language and grammar skills'.

Coaching is about helping others become aware of hidden links and patterns in their own story; and, by appreciating these more clearly, they have more choice about what they can do to become more effective. In this regard, it is clear that there is a real link between appropriate and timely humour and effective coaching.

As coaches, we help our clients to be more agile and responsive to change and to be more effective. How great is it that one of the best tools we have is also one of the most enjoyable. As ever, we must be mindful of the coachee and the conversation must be centred primarily in their experience and interest. Within that framework, there is always scope for appropriate light-heartedness. Here are a few dos and don'ts.

Don't:
- apply face paint or make gorilla noises during a coaching session;
- wear your clothes back-to-front or suggest to the client that they do so 'for a laugh';
- insist that they model the board's group dynamics using a plastic 'potato men' kit and six root vegetables you happen to have in your bag;
- make gurning faces or anything else that might result in your immediate removal to a secure unit.

Do:
- ask yourself how more humour and fun might serve your client in the achievement of their goals;
- appreciate the organisational client context and act appropriately;
- have a few ideas up your sleeve (actually, in context, the potato men idea is not so bad; Lego also make a whole series of characters from knights to cowboys);
- use humour to match and mismatch with your coachee and create energy and fun in your coaching.

3.4 PRESENCE IN COACHING

What does it mean to have *presence* as a coach? While there are many views on what presence actually is (or is not), I think there are three key capacities that people with presence display, whether as a coach, leader, politician or in any other walk of life or profession. They are:

- unconditional positive regard;
- unattached commitment;
- relational agility.

Unconditional positive regard

This is the capacity to hold all other people in a positive light regardless of their background, values, culture or current actions. It doesn't mean agreeing with them or accepting what they do – it is simply the ground of being on which to stand as an acceptance of everyone *as they are* – a human being with their own view of the world, making sense of it as best they can.

In a recent conversation, a friend of mine said to me, 'We're all tiny dots in a great big world.' The implication was that the world 'out there' held meaning and we as individuals sought to find it. I think the reverse is true, that we are each and every one of us a tiny and complete world in a great big dot. We each hold our own meaning in our own unique and personal worldview – it is the great big dot which has no intrinsic meaning.

People with presence hold others in unconditional positive regard as an empathic act of understanding of another's worldview – no matter how bizarre or how at odds with their own it may be. This does not mean being in agreement with the other's worldview, but understanding and appreciating where the other person is – quite literally – in their world.

Unattached commitment

There are never any guarantees in life – being totally committed to success in something does not mean that you will necessarily succeed. It does mean that the odds are highly stacked in your favour but, to quote John Lennon, 'life is what happens when you're busy making other plans'.

Successful people, and those who successfully help others, are those who have relinquished their *need* to succeed. In the letting go of need, they are freed of the burden of disappointment, disillusion, self-doubt, anger, frustration and so on that go with attachment to a particular outcome. This freedom allows commitment to be liberating, energising and fun. It makes commitment not only a means to an end but *an end in itself.* It is focusing not on winning per se, but on playing the very best game, all the time, regardless of circumstance or outcome.

People with presence exhibit a joyous appreciation of the moment, high focus and total confidence – they cannot fail because they have no *need* to win.

Relational agility

We each have the capacity to nurture and support others, as well as challenge and direct them. We can be accepting and allowing, or forceful and push for change. These two poles are referred to as 'Love' and 'Will' and each of us has a preference for either one or the other, regardless of our gender. Some of us feel more comfortable with feelings, following, accepting what is, trusting the existing process and saying less or listening (Love). Others feel more comfortable with thinking, intervening, challenging, creating new process and saying more or telling (Will). Both have clear benefits and downsides: lack of boundaries on the one hand, to over-constraint on the other; low rigour to overplayed challenge; no pressure to make changes to forced change. People with presence exhibit a high degree of agility to move appropriately between the two poles of Love and Will in the best interests of all concerned.

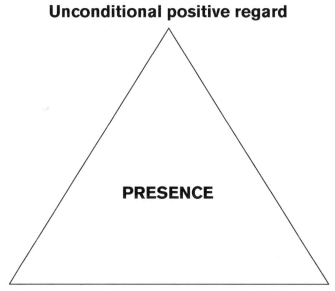

It is the combination of these three capacities that shows up when someone is 'present' for another. This clearly goes beyond mere technique and summarises the learning and development journey of the truly effective coach – and further, of any leader who has enough at stake to enrol the hearts, minds and discretionary effort of those about them. In his recent book *Presence*, Peter Senge quotes the following lines from *I and Thou* by Martin Buber, who captures the essence of 'presence' for the coach:

> *Then he intervenes no more, but at the same time, he does not let things merely happen. He listens to what is emerging from himself, to the course of being in the world: not in order to be supported by it, but in order to bring it to reality as it desires. (p. 144)*

This way of being with another is reflected in Peter Block's classic book *Flawless Consulting*, in which he describes authenticity as a key component of flawless consulting (and one can say the same for flawless coaching):

> *Each act that expresses trust in ourselves and belief in the validity of our own experience, is the right path to follow. Putting into words what you are feeling right now as you work with the client, acting without constraint, without conserving your own experience, is being authentic.*

4 Tools and Techniques

This section describes a number of techniques that the coach can use with a coachee to help them explore their thinking. I have divided them up into three main categories, listed below. As with any tool, its uses are limited only by the imagination of the user. Most of the techniques described below have application in the other two areas, so the categories are for general guidance only:

- *goals* – the long-term end goal and/or the goal for this conversation;
- *awareness* – discovering and examining what is actually going on for the coachee *and* exploring alternative strategies and tactics to move forward;
- *action* – choosing action and commitment to action.

In addition a tool is described for self-coaching ('NIP and TUCK').

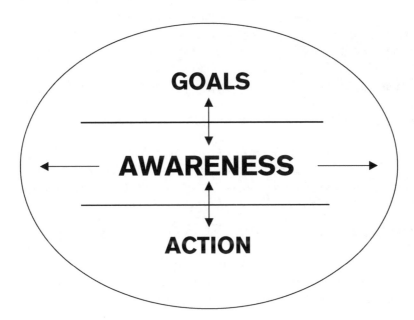

Most of the techniques described contain short sample narratives between coach and coachee. You can assume that all the relevant contracting has been completed and that the level of challenge in the conversation is appropriate.

4.1 TECHNIQUES FOR GOALS

The ideal future: See/Hear/Feel

When you are inspired by some great purpose, some extraordinary project, all your thoughts break their bonds; your mind transcends limitations, your consciousness expands in every direction and you find yourself in a new, great and wonderful world. Dormant forces, faculties and talents become alive and you discover yourself to be a greater person by far than you ever dreamed yourself to be.

— Patanjali, Indian philosopher

In the following dialogue, the coach helps the coachee to move from a negative mindset to a more positive one. Don't agree goals that are negative ('I don't want to be late with the project'), because this tends to be what the mind dwells on; always focus on the positive – the ideal or perfect outcome.

Coach: What do you want to achieve from our work together over the next four months?

Coachee: The project I'm managing is running late and I'm under a lot of pressure from the top not to miss the deadlines. If we miss the deadlines, the customer will demand penalty payments and the boss will come down on me like a ton of bricks. I want to focus on not being late.

Coach: OK, I get that you have tight deadlines and feel under pressure. I'd like you to forget that pressure for a while and focus on the ideal result. What would be the perfect outcome of this project for you?

Coachee: The project would be completed a week ahead of schedule. My team would be upbeat and there'd be bonuses all round. My boss would give me the Malaysian construction project that he promised on the success of this one.

Sometimes the coachee may be too wrapped up in the issue to envisage the ideal future. One very useful technique to help here is 'See/Hear/Feel'. We all have different preferences in the way we express our sense of the world around us. We can be:

- *visual,* preferring to express our world in 'seeing' language:
  - I see your point...
  - I've got the picture...
  - My view is...
  - I don't envisage...

– I don't see how...
– The issue looks tricky...
- *auditory*, preferring to express our world in 'hearing' language:
  – I hear that...
  – That rings alarm bells...
  – The problem sounds like...
  – The issue sounds tricky...
- *kinaesthetic*, preferring to express our world in feeling language:
  – I feel that...
  – My sense of the issue is...
  – I'm grappling with the problem...
  – He's being really tough on me...
  – I tasted success...
  – That went smoothly...
  – The issue feels tricky...

Ask the coachee to express their ideal future by:

- projecting themselves into their ideal future – they are there *now*, so make sure the coachee speaks in the *present tense* to reinforce this sense of time and place;
- describing *very accurately* what they *see*. Ask them to pay close attention to details, such as the time on the office clock, expressions on faces, position of furniture, and so on.
- describing very accurately what they *hear*. How are people expressing themselves in this ideal future? What words are they using, what are they saying?
- describing what they are *feeling* in this ideal future. Pay attention to the coachee's use of language, particularly metaphors.

By listening carefully, the coach can identify the coachee's preferred way of expression and both coachee and coach get a very clear picture or sense of the end goal. Also, it can provide useful milestones to measure progress. For example, if one part of the ideal future is that the coachee is presenting to a major conference, this might indicate some interim learning and development goals around presentation skills. Continuing the coach–coachee conversation from above:

> **Coach:** I'd like to have a better understanding of your end goal. Imagine you're now in your perfect future, in four months' time. What are you seeing around you?
>
> **Coachee:** I've called a team meeting to tell them that we're ahead of schedule. The whole team is there for a change, including Darren, who is always late. It's seven o'clock in the morning, that's early for a meeting. There's coffee in china mugs, not the usual polystyrene rubbish. John is taking the lead and coming up with some new ideas – that's unusual for him... and so on.
>
> **Coach:** And what are you hearing specifically?
>
> **Coachee:** John is being complimentary about his colleagues for a change. I can hear appreciation generally. I can hear my boss congratulating us, although he's not in the room – maybe he's on teleconference... and so on.
>
> **Coach:** And what are you feeling?
>
> **Coachee:** A sense of confidence and a weight off my shoulders. I'm noticing a sense of excitement about the next challenge – the Malaysia project. Which reminds me about the concerns my partner has about what that might mean for us personally.

The coach and coachee now have a clear sense of the ideal future and the coachee can now be clear about their end goal:

- I want the project finished one week ahead of schedule, with the team in good communication with, and appreciation of, each other;
- more communication with the boss by teleconference;
- clarity about my next steps to get the Malaysian project underway and involve my partner in the process of planning, so it works for us both.

Now coach and coachee can begin to work on specific performance goals towards this end goal.

It is possible to take the technique a step further and ask the question 'What do you smell?' It might sound a bit odd, and generally it is not a question I ask, although it can have a very powerful impact for some coachees. If I were coaching a chef who wanted to create their perfect meal, for example, I might well ask them this question as, of course, the sense of smell is particularly sensitive and evocative in their case. The fact is, the sense of smell is an immensely powerful one and often can engage the creative imagination more effectively than the other, more commonly expressed, senses.

CASE STUDY

I was being coached recently in a joint co-supervision exercise with another coaching colleague. I had an issue with a particular executive coaching client – after two sessions I felt our relationship had not developed sufficiently for us to engage in coaching conversations appropriate to the level and importance of the coachee's declared goals.

I was not sure what it was all about and wanted to get clear – for me and for the coachee.

My coaching co-supervisor asked: 'When you are successful in this relationship, what will you see/hear/feel?'

Having answered the question, but not frankly a lot clearer in my own mind, he asked: 'And what will you smell?'

We both laughed and immediately without thinking I replied: 'I will be smelling a cup of freshly brewed coffee right in front of me.'

It was then that the realisation struck me that the coachee was in the habit of having his secretary bring in a cup of coffee (for him) at the start of each session, without offering me one. I started to examine his other little power plays and I soon realised that there was something unspoken in the relationship about the coachee's own issue with retaining control and power, and an inability to let go of the status quo.

That simple cup of coffee enabled me to have a very challenging and direct conversation with the coachee at our next session, from which there arose a deeper relationship and more clarity about how we could move forward appropriately in the coach–coachee relationship.

Listening for metaphors

We all use metaphors as a shortcut to express the way we experience the world. They have unique meaning for each person and allow us to express very succinctly a deep and personal story:

- I feel I'm between a rock and a hard place...
- They'll shoot my ideas down...
- I'm tied to my job...
- I want work to be a bed of roses...
- I need to let go of this need to control my staff...

By listening for metaphor the coach can often pick up on a deep issue very quickly, still mirroring the coachee's own language. In the conversation above, the conversation might continue:

Coach: And what are you feeling?

Coachee: A sense of confidence and a weight off my shoulders. I'm noticing a sense of excitement about the next challenge – the Malaysia project. Which reminds me about the concerns my partner has what that might mean for us personally.

Coach: Tell me about the weight on your shoulders.

Coachee: I feel I've carried it a long time.

Coach: Say some more.

Coachee: I think it's a burden – I'm accountable for this project and the team don't understand what I do for them. I just get it in the neck for their mistakes.

Coach: What do you want to do about this burden?

Coachee: Put it down once and for all.

Coach: What would you have to do to do that?

Coachee: Be more honest about it with the team. Tell them how I feel.

Coach: Would that do it?

Coachee: Not on its own. I'd have to improve my delegation and feedback skills – maybe learn to coach, too!

A new performance goal has now emerged in the conversation. The coach might also notice the coachee's body language reflecting metaphor, for example:

- wringing of hands (feelings of guilt);
- rolling up the sleeves (pent-up energy or frustration);
- cleaning spectacles (wanting an insight about something).

The coach can help the coachee to think laterally by planting a metaphorical idea (e.g. describing the person or relationship as a car, animal, colour, dance, and so on).

Coach: If this problem was say, a car, what would it be and why?

Coachee: Er... that's a weird question! It would be a racing car – too fast for the track, too much noise for the environment, too expensive to keep on the road.

Coach: And the ideal car?

Coachee: Something quieter, cheaper to run and that fits in with the environment.

Coach: You've highlighted three things there: cost, noise and fitting to the environment. Tell me what the problem is costing you ... Tell me more about the noise the problem is making ... Tell me more about the environment that the car needs to fit into ...

The coach's intent is to help the coachee think laterally around the issue and to tease out some of the issues which they can both work with in coaching.

Using pictures

Often, drawing simple pictures can help individuals to express goals and ideas that don't come to them readily in conversation. Here are some ways to access creative thinking using pictures.

- Ask the coachee to draw their goal, then to draw what is stopping them, and finally to draw their picture of success. Tease out the meaning of each picture in conversation with them and the steps they need to take to get from one picture to the next. Then break these steps down into specific actions – some of which will be straightforward and others may need further coaching – and possibly further drawing by the coachee, if you both think it will be helpful.
- Ask the coachee to draw the qualities or skills they bring to their role currently, then to add in a different colour or colours what they need to bring in order to achieve their goals. Discuss the picture, what was added and what their thinking was as they added to the picture. They may have drawn additional links to people, as relationships and communication are often (even usually) the key to success, so be sure to explore these.
- If appropriate, ask the coachee to draw their personal values and discuss these. Then ask them to draw the values of the organisation. What are the differences and similarities? How could these be reconciled?

Pay attention not only to the overall shape of the drawing, but also to the different colours used, the depth of shading and the way the coachee links different parts of the drawing together, all of which can provide insightful material for conversation. Be careful not to interpret any drawings from your own worldview – for example, you may construe that by drawing their boss as a big green giant, that the coachee is somehow afraid of them (it might be simply that they remind the coachee of the 'jolly green giant' associated with a certain brand of sweetcorn). Always ask the question, don't assume. As ever, the real power of the technique lies not in the technique itself – in this case, drawing – but in the coaching conversation that emerges both during and subsequently.

Be sure to have plenty of pens and crayons handy when using drawing techniques with coachees, so their choice of colour, widths and so on is as wide as possible.

Coaching wheels

The intent is to raise awareness around the qualities that the individual perceives as being ideal to perform outstandingly well in that role. The role might be generic, such as team leader, coach, manager, CEO or parent. Alternatively, the role might be functional, such as marketing director, sales manager, production manager or another role where specific functional skills might be required to perform effectively.

By using a simple visual like the wheel, the discrepancies or mismatches between skills can be highlighted visually. The wheel can be referred to in successive sessions to mark progress, and can apply to individual as well as team coaching.

> **Coach:** We agreed last time to look at some of the key qualities you need to do your work effectively. You said you'd do this in consultation with your manager. How did that meeting go? What have you come up with?

- Coach and coachee review the list and, if necessary, reduce it so that it consists of no more than 10 qualities. These qualities become the segments of a pictorial wheel.
- Ask the coachee to score themselves out of 10 (where 1 = low and 10 = high) in terms of their personal effectiveness in each quality. These are noted down as segments of the wheel.
- Now ask them to note a *personal* target score for each quality and a date by when they want that score. As a further piece, they may also want to have a target score for what the *organisation* expects. For example, they may consider themselves at level 4 for negotiation skills and want to achieve a *personal* target of level 8. The *organisation* may only require the individual to have level 5 in negotiation skills.

This will highlight some areas for development which can provide valuable coaching opportunities, as well as discrepancies between the personal aspirations and organisational requirements of the individual.

Note that it is not the point to get an even balance across all the segments of the wheel. The important thing is to focus on what the coachee does well, to help them to *excel* in these areas and to be *good enough* in those other areas where competence is required. This is to focus on strengths. Of course, there may be areas of low competence in which the coachee does need to excel, which might call into question whether the coachee has been given, and taken, training and development opportunities, or even if they are in the right job. This is itself an entirely appropriate subject for coaching.

Example: Ideal qualities for a sales manager
The coachee is a sales manager and has come up with the qualities below. Let's take Good Negotiator as an example:

Coach: Tell me about the quality Good Negotiator.

Coachee: Well obviously in my role it helps to be a great negotiator. I can strike better deals with my clients and maximise profit margins.

Coach: Say a bit about your personal target score of 8. What will your success measures be?

Coachee: I will achieve 20% over target sales and have developed both the Simmons PLC account and the IT to die for PLC account into our top 10.

Coach: You rate yourself at a 4 just now. You want to be at an 8 by the end of the financial year, so you've got around nine months. What do you think you need to learn or develop to move to an 8? Where do you want to start? Which would give you most leverage initially? What would be the biggest learning breakthrough for you? What's the biggest challenge just now?

Coachee: [Allow coachee to respond in full to your questions and ask questions for clarification if necessary.]

Coach: I notice that you rate the organisational requirement target as 7 and you say you want 8. You could aim for the target of 7 and put the extra energy elsewhere, so tell me what is it about a personal target of 8 that appeals to you?

Coachee: I want to be the best sales negotiator in the company. There are special bonuses, but it's also a matter of personal ambition and pride.

Coach: I really get that this is important to you. On a scale of 1 to 10, what is your commitment to achieving this goal?

Coachee: High – say 7.

Coach: What would move that to a 9 or 10?

Coachee: I think it's ambitious and there are specific issues I think will be hard to address, like my relationship with my boss and problems with communication in this company – I may not get the information I need.

Coach: OK, we'll address those one by one. Where do you want to start?

Quality	Current score	Target score	
	Personal	Personal	Organisational
Motivational			
Good listener			
Excellent product knowledge			
Good negotiator	4	8	7
Numerically skilful			
Flexible			
Focused on targets			
Self-starter			

The coach has asked questions to get a sense of what the coachee wants to achieve and to clarify some of the performance issues. Also, the coach has picked up that for the coachee, this is not only about performance, but also pride.

The coach is using the principle of *following interest* by asking the coachee where they want to start, instead of imposing their own view as coach as to where the coach thinks it is best to start. (There is more on using coaching wheels in *Co-active Coaching* by Whitworth et al. – see Bibliography.)

Coaching wheels for teams

Using the same principles as above, coaching wheels can be used with teams. For example, a team 'performance wheel' might consist of elements including:

- level of customer satisfaction;
- targets met;
- targets exceeded;
- feedback from other parts of the business;
- key performance indicators and/or standards of performance;
- delivery times, items shipped, other non-direct sales measures;
- stretch goals or targets;
- specific problems or issues resolved (process or relational), and so on.

A team 'culture wheel' might consist of elements including:

- communication with each other;
- honesty;
- support from other team members;
- feedback from other team members;
- enjoyment;
- challenge;
- inclusion;
- satisfaction;
- achievement;
- a sense of value or purpose, and so on.

Let us use the team sculpture wheel as an example. The first step is for the team to agree on the segments of the wheel. This could be done through a simple round-table brainstorm, gathering all the ideas of elements that the team consider relevant to their 'team culture'. Ensure that everyone has the same understanding of the words used. For example, 'What do we mean by *honesty* in this team?', 'What would *honesty* look or sound like?'

Then allow everyone say, five votes each – they can each choose whether they vote for one element five times (i.e. using all their votes to vote for just one element which is, in their view, very important), or spread their personal votes out, perhaps giving one element three votes and two other elements one vote each, or giving five elements one vote each, and so on). At the end of the process the manager or coach counts the votes and ranks them in order, the top six to eight becoming the segments of the wheel.

The team then privately score the team as they see it on a scale of 1 to 10 against each of the segments. These scores are collected anonymously, averaged out and marked on the wheel, creating the current benchmark for the team. The process is repeated to create a set of scores indicating where the team thinks it should be scoring ideally in those segments, and these are put on the wheel.

There then would ensue a coaching conversation for each segment, discussing questions such as the following.

- What makes us score ourselves at X for this segment?
- What is the current situation regarding this segment for the team?
- What would our goal for this segment (let's say 8) look and sound like?
- What would we be doing differently when we are scoring 8 that we currently don't do?
- What do we need to stop doing/do more of/do less of?
- What has stopped us so far: what are the barriers?
- How can we move forward: what do we need to do immediately/soon or stop doing immediately/soon?
- Who will do what, what help do we need and where will we get it?
- What are the milestones for success?
- When and how will we review progress?

A further development on the anonymised team scoring is to display the personal scores of each team member. While the average benchmarks for current or desired future remain the same, personal opinions and differences can be highlighted. For example, person A may feel that there is already plenty of challenge for the team and does not want to raise the bar much higher, while person B may want to see a lot more team challenge. This raises questions such as the following.

- How can the team raise the bar on challenge in a way that suits every team member?
- What is understood by 'challenge' by each team member, and how is this expressed in their day-to-day work currently?
- How might it be expressed individually in terms of the segment goal?
- How might this difference of opinion affect A and B's relationship?
- How can person A and person B work together effectively with their very differing views on team challenge, and what can other team members do to support them both individually and as a pair?

By adopting this approach for each segment, a very rich seam of personal and team development can be brought to light and then used by the manager or team coach to grow the team and achieve aligned goals.

Team shared support grid

This is a simple and effective way of getting team members to discuss with each other what help they mutually need. The process can be used for any team and in any situation, for example, projects, short- or medium-term planning, specific objectives delivery, and so on. The shaded boxes are for the objectives or needs and the white boxes are for the offers of help and/or support that the other team members can offer that person. Let us take a team consisting of five team members: Jane, Rosinda, Amin, Peter and Harry.

What I can offer: / What I need:	Jane offers:	Rosinda offers:	Amin offers:	Peter offers:	Harry offers:
Jane	Jane's objectives				
Rosinda		Rosinda's objectives			
Amin			Amin's objectives		
Peter				Peter's objectives	
Harry					Harry's objectives

Each team member considers what they need from the other four team members individually and makes a note of these needs or requests in the shaded area which corresponds to their name (for example, Jane enters her objectives or needs in the top-left shaded box which cross-references to Jane/Jane, Rosinda enters her needs and requests in the next diagonal shaded box corresponding to Rosinda/Rosinda, and so on). Each person then has a one-to-one conversation with the others to get clear with the other person exactly what support they can or cannot offer, and what they need from the other. Offers of help are entered in the white boxes across the grid.

Then, the shorthand version of these conversations is captured and shared on a shared support grid. Once the above process is complete, the grid is reviewed by the team as a group to identify duplication, resolve conflicting priorities and align everyone on the next steps. Progress is monitored and reviewed at regular team meetings, the grid is updated appropriately and the process is repeated.

When asking for support from colleagues in this process, consider:
- your customer/end-user – what are they thinking/feeling/wanting?
- your staff – what would give them more involvement or responsibility?
- what isn't happening that would help?
- what is happening that doesn't help?
- what could happen more often, or less often?
- what would speed things up?
- what meetings could be shorter or even dumped?
- what new meetings might be useful and why?
- duplication of effort, are there conflicting priorities?
- where are decisions being made, and is it at the right place or level?
- how staff communicate with each other (relationships and process).

4.2 TECHNIQUES FOR AWARENESS

Language clarity

We all tend to use our language in imprecise ways. I might say: 'There are a number of people involved', when actually I mean: 'There are three people involved'; or 'No one ever listens to me', when actually I mean: 'My line manager didn't appear to respond to my suggestions on the following occasions...'

In this way, we invent stories about our reality and these stories form the basis for our perceptions and subsequent actions. An effective coach will help the coachee to understand the language and story that is shaping their perception and subsequently driving their behaviours and results. It is almost as if we spend most of our time looking at our life through a telescope that is not focused properly. There is a lot of distortion and lack of clarity that gives a false or incomplete picture of what is out there. By focusing and getting clarity in the picture, new understanding and appreciation can emerge. The focus and clarity is achieved through language, and the process is the coaching conversation.

Here is a brief conversation between the coachee and a friend. Notice their language and downbeat tone. The friend is offering advice but this is not helping the coachee to move forward, merely consolidating the coachee's perception of hopelessness in the situation.

Coachee: I'd like some help with a problem.

Friend: Sure, what's up?

Coachee: The sales director has set me higher sales targets than I'd agreed with my sales manager. I'll never meet them in time for the deadline. I don't know what to do.

Friend: That's really tricky – sounds to me like you've been treated very badly. Why don't you talk to the sales manager, maybe negotiate a deal?

Coachee: I've tried that. He's as much under the thumb as I am. Besides, he just does what he's told to do by the sales director. He's pretty useless, really.

Friend: How about speaking directly to her then?

Coachee: No, she's too intimidating – she'd just tell me to get on with it.

Friend: Well, you can only do your best, she won't fire you if you don't meet target, will she?

Coachee: Don't be too sure about that...

Friend: I think you're being over-concerned. I'm sure it's not that bad.

Coachee: You don't work there...

Contrast the above chat with the following coaching conversation, where the coach starts to pick apart the language used by the coachee:

Coachee: I'd like some help with a problem.

Coach: Tell me about it.

Coachee: The sales director has set me higher software revenue targets than I'd agreed with my sales manager. I'll never meet them in time for the deadline. I don't know what to do.

Coach: Let's look at this bit by bit. When did you have the conversation with the sales director?

Coachee: Yesterday morning.

Coach: And how did she actually set you these new targets?

Coachee: Well, she collared me by the coffee machine. She said she'd been looking at the sales figures and we were going to have to increase our software sales by 10%.

Coach: Who are 'we', exactly?

Coachee: The software sales team – there are six of us.

Coach: You said increase sales by 10% – more than what?

Coachee: Well, I assumed she meant 10% more than the budget, but I suppose she could have meant more than last month. She's spoken to my manager about it.

Coach: And what did he tell you?

Coachee: He said that the sales director had spoken to him just before I met her, and had told him about the new targets. It's just our team that's affected, not the hardware sales team. He told me that he'd said it would be tight, but she just said 'Do it anyway.' He doesn't fight his corner.

Coach: How would he fight his corner if he did?

Coachee: Well, he'd push back more by trying to extend the deadline, or reduce the target or get more resources, like the hardware sales manager does, for example.

Coach: So in summary, the sales director has set the whole software sales team and not just you, an increased target of 10%, although you're not clear whether that's against budget or last month. Because of an audit, there's two weeks less time to deliver. You also think your manager doesn't push back enough and negotiate.

Coachee: That's about it.

Coach: How would you like it to be?

Coachee: I'd like my manager to push back and negotiate either an extension or a reduction in the team target. Perhaps we could agree in the team to work out a way to maximise effort on the accounts most likely to produce revenue in the short term to get somewhere near this target.

Coach: OK. What should we focus on today in this conversation that would help you move forward and feel more in control of this situation?

Coachee: I'd like to have a few key questions to ask my manager to get some clarity, as I can see I've made a few assumptions. I'd like a few suggestions to offer him, too.

The coach has probed into the coachee's language, picking up on vague usage or generalised words in order to clarify understanding and get a more objective picture. In particular, by picking up on the vague expression used by the coachee – 'He doesn't fight his corner' – the coach has elicited some specific actions which might help the coachee to refocus on possible opportunities for action. The coach has offered neither sympathy nor advice, but structure and clarity through use of open questions and summary. Note also the future focus towards the end and emphasis on the goal for the conversation.

Pictorial metaphor

(See also 'Using pictures' in the 'Goal' section above.)

Another way of communicating through metaphor is by using pictures. People often find it easier to discuss a picture and the meaning behind the picture, rather than the issue as it relates to them personally. This objectivity allows the coachee to distance themselves from the issue and gain a different perspective.

Ask the coachee to draw:

- their goal;
- their current situation;
- the route they need to take for success;
- what is stopping them;
- how they feel about the situation or relationship, and so on;
- lines of communication.

Tease out the meaning of each picture in conversation with the coachee and the steps they need to take to get from one picture to another.

Ask the coachee to draw the qualities or skills that they bring to their role currently and then to add, in a different colour, what they need to bring in order to achieve their goals. Discuss the picture, what was added and what their thinking was when they added to the picture.

Ask the coachee to draw their personal values, then to draw the values of the organisation. What are the differences and similarities? How could these be reconciled?

Ask the coachee to give you feedback on the session as a drawing, then discuss the picture including the choice and use of colours.

Ask the coachee to imagine themselves in the situation they are describing and to draw, say, a car:

- what type of car are they – why that kind of car (for example, a pick-up truck – room for other people)?
- what kind of a car, or variation on the present car, might be more effective and why (adding a horn to the pick-up truck would get people out of the way – more assertive)?

For car, you can substitute piece of furniture, animal, domestic appliance, bird, and so on. Similarly, ask them what sound or colour best represented them at that time and why.

Ask them to then look at the situation from the viewpoint of a third-party observer and to draw the situation from the observer's perspective. What can the observer say about the situation from their objective viewpoint?

Non-verbals

Words count for fewer than 10% of communication; tone of voice accounts for around 35% and at least 55% is non-verbal behaviour. The coachee's body language will say a lot about their current attitude and state of mind. Also, body language can have a metaphorical interpretation. For example, if the coachee is clenching and unclenching their hands, the metaphorical interpretation might be that they are 'clutching at straws' or desperately clinging on to something that is slipping away from them. (On the other hand, it might be that they have cramp in their hand, so be careful not to jump to conclusions!)

Non-verbal noises may convey deeper meaning, such as the coachee who always preceded everything they said with 'Err... umm...' which we might subsequently discover was a defence mechanism against their lack of self-confidence. It was a symbolic indicator that they could be interrupted by anyone they happened to be talking to and that therefore what they had to say was not that important anyway. (On the other hand, they may have been recovering from a cold and simply clearing their throat.)

By being aware of, and sensitive to, these metaphors in speech and non-verbal behaviour, the coach may add huge depth and richness to their coaching. If the coachee slumps, paces about, avoids eye contact, wrings their hands, runs their hand through their hair, fiddles with items of clothing or pens, it *may* be telling you something. Equally it *may not* – however, being aware of it is the first step, figuring out whether it might mean something is the second, and knowing how to use it appropriately in the coaching conversation is the third.

Listening for either/or dichotomies

In the western world particularly, we are used to thinking in an 'either/or' way. Things are one way or the other, or some shade in between that is still related to one or other of the polarities. It is helpful in coaching (and in life) to believe that there is always a third way that unites 'either/or', and to seek this out. For example, we might regard something as good or bad, or somewhere on a scale between these extremes, such as 'OK' or 'not so great', or 'pretty reasonable', yet this is still polarity thinking as these words continue to reflect the either/or scale:

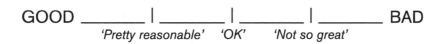

GOOD _____ | _____ | _____ | _____ BAD
       'Pretty reasonable' *'OK'* *'Not so great'*

This and other polarities such as right/wrong, happy/sad, in/out, nice/nasty reflect our general lack of skill in thinking outside of 'two dimensions', compounded by the fact that we don't have the *language* to speak outside of two dimensions. As a result our thinking and speaking in the western world tends to be dualistic. For example, let us assume that there is a position that is neither 'good' nor 'bad', and reflects a completely different third and complementary way of thinking about both good *and* bad. In the figure below and to represent any third way, this is labelled 'commitment'.

Commitment emerges in the *present* moment, while good and bad in this example are both historic concepts in that they reflect beliefs embedded in *past* experience (i.e. up to, but not including, the present moment). Therefore 'commitment' represents a significant and powerful choice point – the coachee can either accept the polarities 'good/bad' as they seem now and the reality that dictates them, or invent a commitment that creates a new reality which the coachee dictates, and therefore gives them new power in the situation.

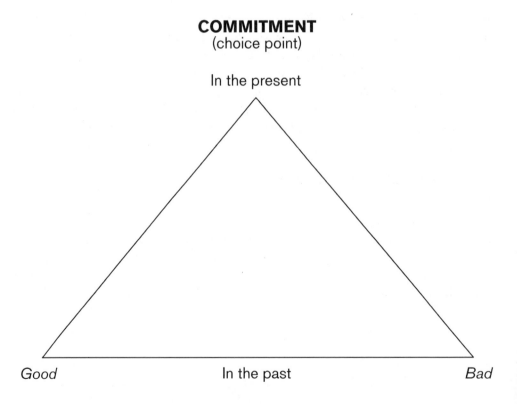

COMMITMENT
(choice point)

In the present

Good   In the past   Bad

Coachee: I have a real dilemma on my hands. Over the last few months I have been getting increasingly angry at this company's lack of environmental care. It seems that they will only do the legal bare minimum to contain pollution and waste. I joined a year ago as sales manager and now the board has asked me to apply for the job of sales director, as the current one is retiring. I need the job for my career progression and income, but from a values standpoint I feel disinclined to accept, as I'd feel I was buying into the board's values. I'm really torn between 'putting up' and risking my job, or just 'shutting up' and accepting both the job and the status quo.

Coach: So let me see if I've got this. You're assuming your choice is either to stay where you are and declare your position on this issue – which you think might cost you your job – or take the promotion and keep quiet about your concerns?

Coachee: That's about it.

Coach: Those are certainly two options. Let me ask you: what are you *really* committed to in this situation? What result would give you most satisfaction and create something different for both you *and* the organisation, rather than just either/or?

Coachee: That I stay and the company changes its approach to environmental issues because of my personal stand.

Coach: On a scale of 1 to 10, where 1 is 'not interested in doing this' and 10 is 'very interested', where are you around this commitment?

Coachee: Yes, I'm interested – maybe a 7.

Coach: What would need to happen to get that commitment to a 9?

Coachee: A real sense for me that I can make this happen and that the company will listen to me.

Coach: So in that context, what would be the ideal outcome for you?

Coachee: That works for me and the company? Well, that in say six months' time, we have a clear environmental policy that is more rigorous than our major competitors. That I am leading a special project to improve our environmental image. Oh yes, and I'm sales director.

Coach: We'll assume you are doing those things in six months' time – how do you feel about the position now?

Coachee: Well, that would be great, but I'm not sure if it's possible.

Coach: OK. Tell me what you see as the barriers to your progress...

The coach clearly restates the issue as an either/or dilemma, then acknowledges the either/or options and seeks to establish a commitment from the coachee. The intention of the commitment is to transcend the dilemma – the coach seeks to check that it is possible, even if it is a stretch target. The coach then clarifies the commitment by creating success measures with the coachee. In this scenario, the coachee is seeing barriers to his progress, but at least now there is a project rather than a problem and the coachee can be in action towards a goal he has clearly identified.

Sculpting

There are a number of ways of using objects in coaching to help the coachee to talk through an issue, relationship or web of relationships. The use of objects removes the personality or personalities from the conversation and allows a more abstract overview.

This exercise is best done spontaneously, using objects conveniently to hand – for example, on the desk or in the desk drawers, in the briefcase (yours, theirs or both), or if you happen to be meeting in a hotel lounge, then whatever items are on the table in front of you: spoons, lumps of sugar, biscuits, cups, saucers and so on. (Do remember that in this latter example, you are in a public place and the chief executive that you are coaching may not wish to be seen sculpting or explaining her executive team dynamics using three ginger biscuits, a pot of coffee and two spoons.) As ever, the coach should be sensitive to the specific needs and desires of the coachee and use any additional techniques such as sculpting with sensitivity, appropriateness and permission.

For example, I was coaching a senior manager who was having some relationship difficulties in his team. After some conversation, which was rather serious and frankly rather depressing, I asked if he would be interested in looking at the issue in a slightly different way, to which he replied that he would. So I got my briefcase and turned it upside-down onto the floor. Out poured a stream of items – pens, markers, sticky notes, map of London, ruler, calculator, small multifunction pen-knife, notepad, some mints and much else besides.

I asked the coachee to choose some items from the pile, one item per team member. As he selected each item, I asked him what had made him choose that particular one to represent the person. For example, he chose the map of London to represent himself and I asked him to explain his thinking:

> *I consider myself to be the route map for the team with a wider overview of the territory, so I can help them see where we're going as a team. Also it's very methodical, specific and directive and a bit creased around the edges – like me!*

This vein of humour grew as the coachee chose other items representing other team members. It was interesting to see him select a particularly barbed blade from the pen-knife to represent the finance director and a small lump of sticky wall-tack representing the operations director, which he carefully placed beneath the blade of the knife! Some things we noted together were:

- the specific items he chose to represent certain individuals, and what this might imply about their perceived personal characteristics and behaviours in the team;
- the spatial relationships between the objects – for example, which were closer, which were elevated or underneath others, which were more distant either from him (as the map) or from others;
- the pattern of the overall model and what it might indicate about team dynamics and relationships between individuals, about his specific leadership style and approach, the stresses in the team and where he might focus his attention to best effect.

He then resculpted the objects into the Ideal Team and we compared the new sculpt with the original – what were the key similarities and differences, what could he do to move from the first sculpt to the second, any particular blocks or impediments, and so on.

This gave a further slant on the situation and began to shape some specific actions which he would take forward to make the team more effective. These included working on his own leadership and communication with specific individuals, being more aware of the relationships between certain team members (particularly the financial director and the operations director), and adapting existing communication processes to be more inclusive.

Perceptual positions: the 'Empty Chair' technique

This is a very useful coaching technique drawn from Gestalt therapy, and a simple and powerful tool for helping the coachee to gain different perspectives about a relationship they want to understand or strengthen, be it a customer, supplier, manager or colleague. The key questions that the coachee needs to be asking themselves are as follows.

- What does this other person think from this viewpoint?
- What is this other person feeling?
- What is this other person wanting?

The 'Empty Chair' technique is a powerful process, so it should only be used with the permission of the coachee, who should understand the purpose and process of the activity. If they say no, don't insist, although you might inquire gently what their reluctance is about. Remember:

- don't hover over the coachee, this is offputting – get down to their level;
- ask a few questions (suggested below), but keep your input to a minimum;
- allow plenty of time for answers;
- the process is intended to help them access their feelings, so make sure the focus is kept to this.

Invite the coachee to position two chairs in a way that reflects the relationship for them now. Let us say that the coachee wants to examine their relationship with a colleague called Peter. Ask the coachee to adopt the following positions.

1. Invite the coachee to sit in one of the chairs and to imagine the other person, Peter, sitting in the other.

What is the situation? What is Peter doing or saying, and how does he look? How does all this make the coachee feel?

2. Invite the coachee to stand, shake loose (in order to dissociate from the previous experience) and sit in the other person's – Peter's – chair and look at their own, now empty, chair. From this perspective, the coachee is sitting in Peter's shoes and looks at the relationship from Peter's point of view.

What is the situation from Peter's standpoint? What does Peter see or hear the coachee do and say? How does the coachee look? How does all this make Peter feel?

3. Now invite the coachee to stand, shake loose again and move to a third standing position a few feet away from the two empty chairs.

What strikes the coachee when they look at the two chairs from here? What is missing from the relationship? If the relationship had a voice, what would it say? What does the coachee want to happen in the future? What insights can this standpoint offer to the coachee?

4. Now shake loose again and move further away still, possibly inviting the coachee to stand on a chair, if possible. Additional height here allows for a 'helicopter' view. From this viewpoint, ask the coachee to look at 'themselves' in position 3.

What resources and capabilities does the coachee have in position 3 that they are not currently using in position 1? Also, from this more distant viewpoint, ask: 'What does the organisation or larger system need from this relationship?'

5. Invite the coachee to return to position 1 and then review the insights they have found from positions 2, 3 and 4. Let them alter the positions of the chairs if they wish. Ask them:
   - how does it feel to be with Peter now?
   - what are you going to do now to make this relationship more effective?

(There is more on this technique in *The Handbook of Coaching Skills* by Jenny Rogers – see Bibliography.)

CASE STUDY

The following is a real example of how a variation of the Empty Chair technique was used in a management situation, recently told to me by a highly experienced senior leader in a uniformed service.

This person, let's call him the Boss, was facing a dilemma. One of his most experienced and popular officers with more than 20 years of unblemished experience had made a simple mistake which had led to a major localised security alert and a potentially dangerous situation. The Boss's senior team were advocating the officer's dismissal for gross negligence to make an example of him, and this would have been a justifiable course of action. On the other hand, the Boss knew that the officer in questions was highly regarded by his work colleagues and his dismissal would have caused a lot of ill-feeling among the staff.

The officer was called to the Boss's office. The Boss was sitting at the desk alone, but in the visitor's chair. The only other available chair in the room was the Boss's own chair, in which the officer was requested to sit. The Boss said:

> Right John, you are now me, with my job, and you now have the task of explaining to me, the Director of Security, exactly how this potentially catastrophic lapse in security could have occurred in the area for which you are accountable.

The Boss continued to play the role of Director of Security, asking tough and searching questions which made the officer understand the ramifications of his actions, and perhaps more importantly made him *feel responsible* for them, as well as the impact that it had had not only on him but on others – specifically, the person in whose chair he was currently sitting, who had the authority to terminate the officer's career with immediate effect.

At an appropriate point in the conversation, the Boss stopped and asked the officer to change chairs. The conversation continued along the lines of:

> Now you know what it's like to be in my shoes and in my chair and I want you to remember that. The incident is now closed. You can go.

The next day there was a knock at the Boss's door and the same officer was ushered in. He said:

> Boss, I didn't sleep a wink last night. I've been in this job for over 20 years and I've had a lot of tickings off in my time from a lot of very hard managers, and I can tell you that yesterday was the worst by far – I feel terrible about what happened and I personally promise you that it will never happen again.

The Boss's simple use of perceptual positions had made the officer not only understand the Boss's viewpoint, but had helped to create in him a 'felt shift', which is the hallmark of significant attitudinal and behavioural change.

4.3 **TECHNIQUES FOR ACTION**

Immediate mentors

Sometimes, people are very stuck in their situation and cannot think of what next steps to take, even after coaching for raised awareness. Pursuing this with questions such as 'What can you do now?', 'What else can you do?', 'What haven't you done yet but want to do?' or 'What are you afraid to do?' can simply reinforce the individual's sense of 'stuckness'.

The 'immediate mentor' is a simple model to move beyond this stuckness. We all know people whose advice we would respect and trust. They might be parents, relatives, friends, colleagues, teachers, coaches, consultants, religious advisers or authors whose books have inspired or helped us. What advice would one or more of these people offer to the coachee in the situation they now find themselves?

- Ask the coachee to think of three or four 'mentors' – people whose advice on this matter they would respect and trust. They may only decide on one mentor, or want more than four – however, beware having a roomful, it can get confusing keeping track. Three or four is usual, five is the likely limit.
- Ask the coachee to imagine the mentors they choose are sitting in the room with them. Where are they each sitting in respect to the coachee?
- Ask the coachee to select one of the mentors and to describe them physically. The purpose of this is to 'bring them into the room' and to make it easier for the coachee to identify with the advice given. Ask why they chose this person as a mentor for this problem.
- Now ask the coachee to imagine what the mentor would advise them to do. Repeat this process for each of the selected mentors.
- When the coachee has received advice from their chosen mentors, bring the focus of the conversation back to just you – the coach – and the coachee. Ask them to summarise the advice they have been given and what action would they now be prepared to take. Check that this action is appropriate to the goal for the session.

In this technique, although the individual often feels that they have been offered valuable advice, the fact is, the advice they are acting upon is their own. They have not been told by anyone – certainly not by the coach – what to do, and so the solution remains their own.

Coach: Your goal for this conversation was to find a way of improving your relationship with your boss. We've discussed a number of issues [summarise] and you are very clear that you must take some action in the next week. You've considered a number of options [summarise] which you've discounted. What else could you do?

Coachee: I don't know – I'm stuck.

Coach: OK, let's imagine that you've invited three or four special advisers to help you with this. Whose advice would you respect and value on this issue? Think about anyone you know or know of who might be able to help.

Coachee: Well, there's Frank – he's a peer at work and is always full of good, sound ideas. And there's Ellen, my wife.

Coach: Can you describe them a little? Imagine they are both sitting with us in the room now – where would they be sitting in relation to you? Whose advice would you like to ask for first?

Coachee: Oh, definitely my wife's – she'd never let me listen to Frank anyway!

Coach: What advice can Ellen offer you now about this situation?

Coachee: I think she'd say to get more involved personally with the boss – maybe go out for a drink after work or something. Break the ice a bit.

Coach: What else might she advise?

Coachee: Well, I know she'd say to me to be more assertive with him – not always say 'yes' when it might affect special weekend plans, for example.

Coach: What about Frank?

Coachee: Oh, he'd definitely tell me to be more assertive with the boss.

Coach: So they're both telling you to be more assertive? In what particular situations? How would they know you were taking their advice – what would they see or hear?

The coachee now describes the action or actions which they have been 'advised' to take by their mentors in the conversation. Hopefully this will lead to some specific commitment to act once the intended outcome and success criteria are agreed between coach and coachee.

The benefit of hindsight

In this simple technique, the coach encourages the coachee to put themselves into the ideal future, now that the goal has been achieved, and to describe clearly the circumstances of success. The coach then asks the coachee to look back over the imaginary journey they have travelled to reach this successful place. Now, with the benefit of hindsight, ask the coachee the following questions.

- What were the key milestones on this journey to success?
- How long has it taken?
- What was the best thing to happen or the hardest circumstance to overcome?
- How did they overcome obstacles that got in their way?
- What help have they had on the way and from whom?
- What have been the risks and hindrances?
- What did the coachee do to minimise these?
- What have been the most memorable moments?
- What was the one thing that made the biggest difference in achieving the goal?

Now bring the coachee back to the present time. With the benefit of this hindsight, what can they now see that they could do to move forwards to the goal? Using the coachee's answers to these questions, you can build a set of specific measurable milestones towards success and then help the coachee to begin that journey.

Coach: Let's go back to your goal for this session. You said that you wanted to have at least the first few points of an action plan to have better communication in your team, as you think improving communication will improve customer service?

Coachee: Yes – from our conversation, that does seem to be the most important thing to focus on now. It's especially crucial as the customer service team is split between three local sites.

Coach: Imagine you have achieved your goal and you now have really effective team communication. Tell me how that looks and sounds.

Coachee: Well, we're all in one site for a start, so we can talk together easily as one team and offer mutual support in a way we haven't before. We've got the new telephone system running smoothly at last and everyone trained in its use. We've got the three extra staff we needed and we are exceeding call performance targets by five per cent, so we're all expecting a bonus!

Coach: What else tells you you've been successful? [Coachee describes further.]

Coach: What's the timeframe been?

Coachee: About six months or so.

Coach: And what have been the key milestones?

Coachee: Getting everyone proficient with the new system – it's not just the training – people have needed time and coaching to become used to the new software package. So proficiency is one milestone and the other key one is having the whole team in one place.

Coach: Are these goals – moving offices and proficiency – both realistically achievable in the timeframe?

Coachee: Yeah, it's all on the cards anyway, but the sooner I can make it happen, the better the communication issue will be.

Coach: So which one of those – office moves and proficiency – stands out for you just now? [Following interest]

Coachee: Having the whole team together, without a doubt. In the future, I envisage we're all in the new building, which is more open plan and designed for IT cables, so the work environment is much better.

Coach: So, tell me what you did to get the team into the new building – remember, it's already done, so just tell me what you had to do to achieve this result.

Coachee: I had to convince my boss the sales director that it would be beneficial, as she was against it for logistical reasons, and it meant she had to persuade Finance to move out. I also had a bit of a battle with Janice, the leader of one of the teams that needed to move, as she hates working open plan. And of course I had to consult with all three teams to work out the best way to do the move and what the problems might be.

Coach: Which of those – persuading the sales director, the battle with Janice and team consultation – holds your attention at the moment? [Following interest]

Coachee: Team consultation – I need to paint a picture that will help them all to see how much better this will be for us all, and then ask them for their support.

Coach: Tell me more about the consultation process you've envisaged...

The coachee has created a picture of the future from which they can look back at the steps they have taken. The coach has helped the coachee by structuring the conversation so that it becomes increasingly focused on specific points as the coach follows the interest of the coachee, leaving choice in the conversation with the coachee at all times.

Scaling

Scaling is a simple technique that encourages coachees to look at the gaps between where they are now and where they want to be, or to what they have committed. The two main applications of scaling are as follows.

The first is in measuring commitment during the Will or Way forward part of the To GROW model (see p. 34). At this point in a coaching session, the coach will need to understand the commitment the coachee has to get into action (no action = no result). Here are a few questions that help the coach to appreciate where the coachee is in the scheme of things.

- What's your commitment (on a scale of 1 to 10)?
- What's missing that has you score your commitment level under 9?
- How could you move your commitment nearer to 10?
- Now could you adjust your identified actions that would have your commitment to action nearer to 10?

Part of the process is to help remove obstacles to action by allowing the coachee to explore what is holding them back from a 9 or 10 commitment. For example, if the coachee says that their commitment is a 6, explore with them what they could do differently or alter in their committed actions that would then move them towards a 9.

It is far better that the coachee has slightly less action to take and does what they commit to at the end of a coaching session, than for the coach to find out later that the coachee never intended to take a particular action at that point because something was holding them back that they did not mention at the time.

The second is in creating a more solution-focused approach to action (this technique is explained in detail in *The Solutions Focus* by Jackson and McKergow – see Bibliography). The technique involves the following.

- Ask the coachee to think ahead to when the issue or problem is perfectly resolved (for this process, see the 'Ideal Future' technique on page 90).
- Assuming that future is a 10 on the scale, where are they now? (The coachee scales from 1 to 10.)
- Say, for example, the coachee says that they are at 3 or 4 out of 10 – ask them to appreciate what they have done, or are doing, that makes them say 3 or 4 out of 10 rather than 1 or 0. This helps the coachee to think through all the positive elements of their situation and actions to date rather than dwell on the problem or negatives.
- Ask what actions they could take to move them from where they are now on the scale (e.g. 3 or 4) up one or two points on the scale (e.g. to a 5 or 6). Again, this focuses on what they could more of that they are already doing, rather than focusing on less of or negatives.
- Finally, clarify the coachee's commitment to action at the end of the coaching session.

Self-coaching using the 'NIP and TUCK' model

Self-coaching is simply a process for thinking through a problem or issue in a more detached and logical way. By definition, this process is one you do on your own. The more you coach, the more you will find a tendency to self-coach and to be more structured and focused in your thinking. Self-coaching cannot match the benefits of being in dialogue with a coach, but you can still achieve a lot by using the process alone.

The NIP and TUCK model for self-coaching is that our experience gives a clear structure for raising personal awareness, marshalling thoughts and gaining some objectivity around a problem.

The NIP process is all about gathering as much data as objectively as possible, trying to avoid interpretation, and the TUCK process is about using the data to move forward.

- *Notice* what's occurring in the moment – what are your thoughts, feelings and sensations? Be as objective and non-judgemental as possible;
- get *Interested* in what you notice – relax and focus on the here and now;
- *Pose questions* – what does this data tell you about:
  - your situation or the physical circumstances;
  - your behaviours;
  - the capabilities or skills you are bringing to the situation;
  - the beliefs you hold about the situation;
  - the story you are telling yourself about who you are in this situation.

With this data, you can then:

- *Take stock* of the situation objectively, get a 'helicopter' perspective;
- *Understand* what is stopping you – in you, in others, in the environment;
- *Choose* alternative strategies and weigh them up; look at the pros and cons;
- *Keep going* – no action means no results.

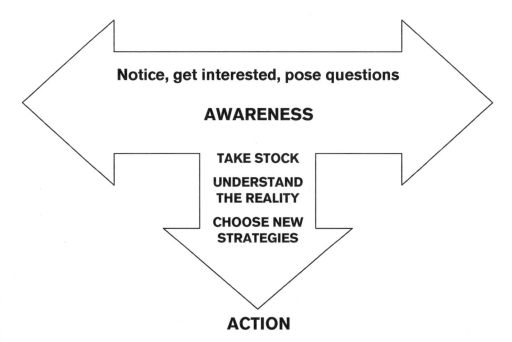

Notice, get interested, pose questions

AWARENESS

TAKE STOCK

UNDERSTAND THE REALITY

CHOOSE NEW STRATEGIES

ACTION

Self-coaching using the To GROW model

Another self-coaching process is simply to use the To GROW model as a paper-based exercise. Simply write down a few questions under each phase of the model and think through your answers to each in turn.

Goal:

- What do I want to achieve specifically?
- How will I know I have succeeded?
- What is the timeframe?
- What are my success measures or criteria?
- What baby steps or milestones are there on the way?
- Is the goal realistic and achievable?
- What can I realistically do and not do in the timeframe?

Reality:

- What have I done so far?
- What effect did this have?
- What am I doing now?
- What is stopping me – what am I afraid of?
- Who else is involved or could be involved?
- What is happening inside or outside my control?
- What does my intuition tell me about the situation?
- What impact will success have on me or others?
- What might I have to risk or give up?

Options:

- What could I do now?
- and what else...? ...and what else...?
- If I had no constraints...
- If I was in complete control and answerable to no one...
- What would a respected friend or colleague advise me to do?
- Looking back, having reached my goal, what one or two things did I do that made the difference?

Will/Way forward:

- What am I going to do now specifically and by when?
- What is my commitment on a scale of 1 to 10? If fewer than 8, what might bring it to an 8 or more?
- What can I really commit to, to help me achieve my goal?
- What might stop me in action – what can I do to minimise that?
- What help do I need and where can I get it?

Self-coaching is usually less effective than one-to-one coaching as there is no 'outsider' to challenge your assumptions or thinking process. This is the power of a coaching dialogue which is not available to the self-coach. It takes a high degree of self-awareness and commitment to self-coach effectively, although it is a skill which can be developed very successfully over time.

Bibliography

REFERENCES

Balakrishnan, A, 'Iraq? They Just Need to Think it Through', 24 April 2007, online at: http://education.guardian.co.uk/higher/profile/story/0,,2063752,00.html

Block, P, *Flawless Consulting*, Jossey-Bass/Pfeiffer, 1981.

Bohm, D, *The Essential David Bohm*, Routledge, 2003.

Bruner, J, 'Research Currents: Life as Narrative', *Language Arts*, 1988, 65(6).

Champy, J, *Re-Engineering Management: The Mandate for New Leadership*, Harper Business, 1995.

Clarke, A, *Pattern Recognition Theory of Humour*, Pyrrhic House, 2008.

de Geus, A, *The Living Company: Habits for Survival in a Turbulent Business Environment*, Harvard Business School Press, 1997.

Downey, M, *Effective Coaching*, Thomson Texere, 2000.

Einstein, A, 1950, 'Letter to the Editor', *New York Times*, 29 March 1972.

Forrest, A, *Five Way Management*, The Work Foundation, 1998.

Gallwey, T, *The Inner Game of Tennis*, Pan, 1974.

Gallwey, T, *The Inner Game of Work*, Orion Business Books, 2000.

Holland, J. 'It's Funny You Think That', *The London Newspaper*, 19 July 2007.

Heber, P, 'Letter to the Editor', *National Geographic*, March 2008.

Jackson, PZ and McKergow, M, *The Solutions Focus*, Nicholas Brealey Publishing, 2002.

Jarvis, J, 'The Rise and Rise of Coaching', *Coaching at Work*, CIPD, October 2005.

Jaworski, J, *Synchronicity: The Inner Path of Leadership*, Berrett Koehler, 1996.

Lloyd, M and Rothwell, B, *Leadership 101*, Directory of Social Change, 2007.

Pirsig, R, *Zen and the Art of Motorcycle Maintenance*, Bodley Head, 1974.

Proctor, B, 'Supervision: A Co-operative Exercise in Accountability', in M Marken and M Payne (eds) *Enabling and Ensuring: Supervision in Practice*, National Youth Bureau, Council for Education and Training in Youth and Community Work, 1986.

Matisse, M, *Matisse on Art* (ed. JD Flam), University of California Press, 1995.

Rogers, J, *Handbook of Coaching Skills*, Open University Press, 2004.

Scott-Peck, M, *The Different Drum: Community Making and Peace*, Simon and Schuster, 1987.

Senge, P, Scharmer, CO, Jaworski, J and Flowers, BS, *Presence: Exploring Profound Change in People, Organisations and Society*, Nicholas Brealey Publishing, 2005.

Tuckman, B, 'Developmental Sequence in Small Groups', *Psychological Bulletin*, 1965, 63, 384–99.

Wiseman, R, 'Smile Experiment Gauges Intuition' quoted in BBC News (Scotland) 1 April 2005, online at: http://news.bbc.co.uk/1/hi/scotland/4397743.stm

Wheatley, M, *Leadership and the New Science*, Berrett Koehler, 1996.

Whitmore, J, *Coaching for Performance*, Nicholas Brealey Publishing, 1996.

Whitworth, L, Kimsey-House, H and Sandahl, P, *Co-active Coaching: New Skills for Coaching People Toward Success in Work and Life*, Davies Black, 2003.

Zukav, G, *The Dancing Wu Li Masters: An Overview of the New Physics*, Rider Hutchinson, 1979.

FURTHER READING

Goss, T, *The Last Word on Power*, Piatkus, 1996.

Hargrove, R, *Masterful Coaching*, Jossey Bass, 1995.

Hawkins, P and Smith, N, *Coaching, Mentoring and Organisational Consultancy*, McGraw-Hill, 2006.

Hill, P, *Concepts of Coaching*, ILM Publishing, 2005.

Kline, N, *Time to Think*, Ward Lock, 1999.

Satir, V, *People Making*, Souvenir Press, 1972.

Scott-Morgan, P, *The Unwritten Rules of the Game*, McGraw-Hill, 1994.

Senge, P, *The Fifth Discipline: The Art & Practice of the Learning Organization,* Nicholas Brealey, 1994[1990].

WEBSITES OF COACHING BODIES IN THE UK

This list is for information only and is not necessarily an endorsement of any particular organisation.

European Mentoring and Coaching Council (EMCC) (www.emccouncil.org)

The EMCC exists to promote good practice and the expectation of good practice in mentoring and coaching across Europe. This pan-European council consists of representatives from several national EMCCs plus direct members in countries where a local EMCC does not yet exist.

International Coach Federation (www.coachfederation.org.uk)

The International Coach Federation is a professional association for personal and business coaches worldwide. With more than 12,000 members, it is currently the largest professional coaching association in the world. It has a commitment to developing coaching excellence, helping to establish a career structure for coaches through its three levels of credentials and helps people find the right coach for their needs.

Association for Professional Executive Coaching and Supervision (www.apecs.org)

The Association for Professional Executive Coaching and Supervision is the professional body providing standards and accreditation for executive coaching and the supervision of executive coaches. It also provides good practice guidance and information about coaching and supervision.

Association for Coaching (www.associationforcoaching.com)

The aims of the Association for Coaching are to advance education and best practice in coaching, to develop and implement targeted marketing initiatives to encourage growth to the industry, to promote and support development of accountability and credibility across the industry, and to encourage and provide opportunities for an open exchange of views, experiences and consultations.

British Psychological Society (BPS) (www.bps.org.uk/coachingpsy)

The special subgroup in coaching psychology (part of the BPS) was established to provide psychologists who are members of the BPS with an effective means of sharing research and practical experiences that relate to the psychology of coaching. Also joining are a growing number of non-psychologist coaches interested in the appropriate application of psychological theory and methods to coaching practice. Coaches who are not psychologists are welcome to join the group, provided that they become affiliate members of the BPS.

Index